D1554020

"Although each story is unique, you ˅ by the short stories written by the ch spective on the events of September children are tomorrow's heroes, capable of positively impacting our world for the good of others."
Doug MacMillan, Executive Director
Todd M. Beamer Foundation, Inc.

"Will we ever get over the day America cried? All those questions and concerns we have—will they ever be answered? Will we ever forget? While reading this book, *911: The Day America Cried,* I realized we will never forget 911. This book is so warm and touching—you may find it hard to complete at first, but you will definitely force yourself to do so. Many of us felt guilty as we went along with our daily routines and tried to pretend such a horrid event never happened, but this book reminds everyone that it *did* happen, and we must never forget those people and heroes we lost for our country. *The Day America Cried* touched my heart as a person and a mother. And as a writer, well…I am speechless. GOD BLESS AMERICA, AND WE WILL SURVIVE!!"
Susan Younan Attiyah, author of
I'll Never Find Anything in Here!

"This book is a true tribute to the heroic actions of countless Americans who gave their lives...It will have you in tears, but more importantly, it will leave you with a renewed sense of what it means to be an American—what it means to have freedom of speech, freedom to do as one pleases, and freedom to sleep at night, knowing for the most part, that our children are safe because of courageous men, such as Todd Beamer. Yes, I'm proud to be an American."
Alyice Edrich, Editor
TheDabblingMum.com Online Magazine

"On September 11, 2001, terrorists brought America to her knees. The frightening shock of that day will remain etched in the minds of people worldwide forever. And on bended knee, we prayed. Then victoriously, America picked herself up and stood proud. The American people stood tall and united. The flag waved free. *911: The Day America Cried* immortalizes the raw emotions and heartfelt feelings of Americans all across our great nation in the aftermath of the tragedy and pays tribute to the indomitable American spirit."

      Tina L. Miller, Motivational Speaker,
      Editor in Chief of *Obadiah Magazine,* and
      Author of *When A Woman Prays*

911:
The Day America Cried

A Collection of Poems,
Letters, and
Stories on an American
Tragedy

Compiled by Victoria Walker

Obadiah Press

607 N. Cleveland Street
Merrill, Wisconsin

1826 Crossover Road, PMB 108
Fayetteville, Arkansas

911: The Day America Cried
Copyright ©2002 Obadiah Press

Published by Obadiah Press in cooperation with WordWalker Publishing

Compiled by Victoria Walker
Preliminary editing by Victoria Walker

Cover photo and design by Kymberli W. Brady
Copyright ©2002 Kymberli W. Brady. Used with permission.

Page layout and final editing by Tina L. Miller

ISBN: 0-9713266-5-7

Printed and published in the United States of America

This book is dedicated
to America and her allies—
in hope that freedom
will continue to ring
for us all.

Table of Contents:

5. LETTERS AND PRAYERS:
TO HEAL A NATION 169

Acknowledgments

*9*11: The Day America Cried would not exist without the support and encouragement of many people who have touched my life. Each of us becomes the person we are through the many people and experiences we encounter during our lifetime. My heartfelt gratitude goes out to the people who have touched my life:

My son, Jeremy Walker—I hope you will always cherish the fact that you were born in the greatest country on this earth—never take your freedoms for granted. In America, you can accomplish any goal and attain any dream…never stop reaching for yours.

My parents, Averitt and Rhonda Walker—For your support and encouragement and for raising me to believe that I could accomplish my dreams. (And for putting up with me all these years.)

My brother and sister-in-law, Phillip and Carla Butler—For always being supportive and for being the best brother and sister-in-law that anyone could ask for.

My grandmother, Pearl Dennis—For teaching me to speak my mind, just as you do!

My grandfather, Gene Dennis—For his bravery, along with the thousands of other soldiers who have fought to defend this great country. We can never thank all of you enough for the sacrifices you made and for preserving the freedoms that we all sometimes take for granted.

My cousin and best friend, Shannon Walker—For always being there—through the best of times and the worst of times. Thanks for always listening and always offering to help. Just like our dads before us, we will remain the best of friends until the end.

For all of my family: the Walkers, the Dennises, and the Kirkpatricks—I am blessed to have you all. There is nothing more important than family. I love you all.

Kymberli Brady—Your generosity has amazed me more than once. I can never thank you enough for the wonderful cover you created for this book and for all the help you gave me in making this book a reality.

Sue Shackles—For helping me select the perfect stories for this book and for always having the time to help.

Shelle Castles—For being a wonderful friend. You've helped me more than you know! I'm still waiting to see that book in print!

Holly N. LiCalzi and The Todd Beamer Foundation—For agreeing to partner with us to help the victims of September 11. Lisa Beamer, you are truly an inspiration. The world could use more people like you.

Tina Miller and LaDonna Meredith, my publishers—Thank you for sharing my dream of making this book a reality. It never would have happened without you and Obadiah Press. I greatly appreciate your guidance and your never-ending patience with my never-ending questions. May God continue to bless you and Obadiah Press.

To all the members of my favorite writing group,

Momwriters.com—Thank you all for your encouragement and guidance. You are all an inspiration!

To all the contributors—You are the heart of this book. I can't thank you enough for sharing your heartfelt words on a subject that is not easy to talk or write about. Thank you for allowing your feelings to speak so eloquently.

To all the young writers who contributed to this book—Your forthright honesty and emotion is priceless. Never stop reaching for your dreams; never give up hope in America or in your fellow Americans.

To the Heroes of America—Those that gave their lives on September 11 and on many other days in history to help their fellow man and to preserve the liberties of this great country.

And most of all, thanks to God for all of His blessings.

May God continue to bless each one of you. And may He continue to bless America.

— *Victoria Walker*

Foreword

September 11. The mere mention of that date conjures up a nightmare of images that we all wish we had never witnessed: images of airplanes crashing; buildings falling—killing thousands of innocent people; terrified victims jumping to a certain, horrible death from the World Trade Center towers to avoid a certain, possibly more horrible death of being burned alive. Mothers, fathers, and children lost. Families destroyed. Hearts broken. A nation under siege. Fire. Smoke. Fear. Tears. Death. Destruction. Terrorism. War. Horrible images burned into our minds—scenes that can never be erased.

Prior to September 11, I, like most Americans, felt safe, almost smug in my American citizenship. Images of war and destruction flashed across my television screen, but those images were worlds away, in another country that I'd never been to and, in some cases, never heard of. They didn't affect me; those things could never happen here—never in America! I was certain that no one was daring enough, or crazy enough, to wage an attack on American soil. But someone was. Our nation was forever changed because someone was!

The stories and poems in this book will cause some of the images from September 11 to resurface. Some stories may bring more tears, while others will bring hope.

Maybe images so powerful should not be forgotten, no matter how agonizing it might be to remember. Perhaps we should not allow ourselves to forget or to become too complacent with our freedom or our security.

The horrible images of September 11 will be carried with each of us for the rest of our lives. Those images are in the back of our minds, tucked away—*but always there.*

But out of despair, comes hope. Along with those devastating images, another collection of images arose—images that represent the true spirit of our nation. The images I choose to focus on are these: Hope. Healing. Love. Unity. Prayer. God. Patriotism. Heroes. America. Freedom. Peace. May these be the images that continue to touch our nation and our lives. May God continue to bless America, today and always.

—Victoria Walker

The
Todd M. Beamer
Foundation

Proceeds from the sale of this book will benefit The Todd M. Beamer Foundation. The authors who contributed their stories to this book have unanimously decided to donate any royalties from the sale of this book to which they would otherwise have been entitled to The Todd M. Beamer Foundation.

It is our hope that the faithful, heroic legacy of Todd M. Beamer will live on in the hearts and minds of Americans through the work of this foundation. Todd M. Beamer is one of many heroes who emerged on September 11, 2001, when he and other passengers tried to regain control of United Airlines Flight 93 after it had been hijacked by terrorists. The last words an airfone operator overheard him say: "Are you ready? Let's Roll!" will be etched in the minds of many Americans forever.

The Todd M. Beamer Foundation is a nonprofit organization created to help meet the long-term needs of the children who lost parents in the events of September 11, 2001, to assist future victims of terrorism, and to continue Todd's passion for mentoring and equipping youth to make the same heroic choices he made throughout his life.

To make an additional contribution to The Todd M. Beamer Foundation, visit www.BeamerFoundation.org or write to: Todd M. Beamer Foundation, P.O. Box 32, Cranbury, NJ 08512

For stock contributions, contact William Beatty at 1-866 BEAMER 23 or wbeatty@beamerfoundation.org

Introduction

The events of September 11, 2001, will be commemorated forever—in history books, in our memories, and in our hearts.

September 11, 2001, truly is the day America cried—and much of the world cried with her. It was a day marked with tragedy, intense grief and mourning, fear, courage, despair, and yet also…hope. It is a day few will ever forget.

It is my hope that this book will do several things:

First, that it will help us commemorate a day in history, a day marked by tragedy and grief, but also by heroes and courage—a day that began with an act of terrorism born out of an enemy's hatred for America but backfired in the face of that evil intent when Americans of all races and colors were united in the bonds of love, compassion, and patriotism.

Second, that it will serve as a reminder to all of us and to future generations so that such a fate may never befall our nation again—that never again will we allow ourselves to become complacent and as such, an easy target for evil. And that we will recognize that the freedom we all hold so dear comes at a price—a price that many Americans have paid throughout our history—and that we will honor our veterans who served in all branches of the armed forces and the protective services. They are heroes *every* day, and there are untold other American heroes out there, too—who do not wear uniforms yet still stand up for our freedom in their own ways.

Third, that this book will enable each of us to come to peace with that day as we relive it and so begin or continue the process of healing—as individuals, as grieving families and friends, and as a nation. We are one nation united under God.

May God grant us His beloved peace and mercy and help us to carry on.

Through the words of the writers who wrote to express their emotions in the midst of and the aftermath of this infamous date—the pain, frustration, fear, grief, confusion, pride, and love—you will be moved, possibly to tears, as I was. Their words echo the thoughts, feelings, and prayers—both spoken and unspoken—in the hearts of Americans and our allies all over the world in the aftermath of September 11, 2001. If the tears come, let them. Remember—it's OK to cry. Tears facilitate healing. Let them wash away the pain.

The stories and poems included deliberately reflect a diversity of people—of many faiths, backgrounds, races, ethnic histories, and ages; and a diversity of emotions and opinions about what to do in the aftermath of September 11, 2001; how to heal our hurting hearts; and how to best defend our nation against further attacks. While the perspectives may be different, the emotions are real, and each and every story is inspiring in its own right.

This book was born of a tragedy, but it is offered in the spirit of hope—the hope that we will continue to come together as a people, in love and in compassion—to become one—one nation under God, indivisible, with liberty and justice for all.

Tina L. Miller
Author of *When A Woman Prays*
Editor in Chief, Obadiah Press

1

September 11, 2001

"Freedom itself was attacked this morning and I assure you freedom will be defended."

— President George W. Bush

The Heroes of Flight 93:
Interviews with Family, Friends Detail the
Courage of Everyday People

By Kim Barker, Louise Kiernan and Steve Mills
Chicago Tribune

They waited, the way people wait on a plane. You can picture them spreading out inside this mostly empty flight to San Francisco, the smokestacks and cranes of the Newark skyline looming outside their windows.

You can hear them working their cell phones, calling their friends, their offices.

For 41 minutes they waited on the tarmac to take off. Two pilots, five flight attendants, and 37 passengers. Among them, four men knew they were all waiting to die.

When United Flight 93 finally took off, it began a journey that would end not in San Francisco, as planned, or by smashing into some Washington target, but in an aching glory.

Since September 11, the story of the passengers who fought their hijackers on Flight 93 has become an icon of good thwarting evil, a story of sacrifice and courage that a nation has embraced in a time of fear and uncertainty.

No one will ever know exactly what happened on that plane. But new interviews with the family, friends, and co-workers of passengers who made last-minute calls give a more complete account of their desperate struggle.

At the same time, questions emerge about the role of the fourth hijacker and raise the possibility that instead of a single plot to overcome the terrorists, passengers and flight attendants in different parts of the plane may have hatched separate plans. While most attention has focused on a group of tall, athletic men who apparently planned to rush the hijackers, at least one flight attendant told her husband she was boiling water to use as a weapon.

The clues from the wreckage are small: a knife concealed inside a cigarette lighter, a manual of prayers and instructions written in Arabic, a cockpit-voice recorder, still under analysis, that reportedly holds a garble of American and Arabic voices.

But the key to whatever took place on Flight 93 may be in the 41 minutes it sat on the ground.

It gave the passengers enough time to hear about the three other hijacked planes that smashed into the World Trade Center and the Pentagon that morning.

The delay took the plane off the precise schedule the terrorists had likely relied upon and put it on one that gave the passengers and crew knowledge—knowledge that incited them to fight back and to say goodbye to loved ones before the jet plunged into a reclaimed strip mine in Pennsylvania, taking with it everyone aboard.

It was 5 a.m. Tuesday and still dark when Deborah Welsh's husband carried her bag down the stairs of their second-floor walkup in Hell's Kitchen in New York.

Welsh, who had been a flight attendant for more than 25 years, usually avoided early-morning flights, but she had agreed to trade shifts with another worker.

Her husband, Patrick, wasn't even sure where she was going when she set off for the bus, wearing her uniform and the navy cap that he jokingly said made her look like the sailor on the Cracker Jack box.

At a friend's home in New Jersey, public-relations executive Mark Bingham, scrambling to pack his old college rugby duffel bag after oversleeping the 6 a.m. alarm, forgot his belt.

Nicole Miller, carrying a purple backpack stuffed with her textbooks, set off with her boyfriend, Ryan Brown, hoping to switch their separate flights back to California so they could fly together.

And so it began, people making their way to Newark International Airport, Terminal A, Gate 17.

There was the Japanese college student and the German wine expert. The refuge manager for the Fish and Wildlife Service flying home from his grandmother's 100th birthday party. The *Good Housekeeping* magazine marketer on her way back from her grandmother's funeral.

There was the advocate for the disabled who stood less than four feet tall and carried herself like a giant. The retired restaurant worker flying to San Francisco to claim the body of his son who had been killed in a car crash on his honeymoon. The toy company executive who sported a Superman tattoo on his shoulder.

Almost one-third of the people on Flight 93 were there by the slimmest of chances: cancellations, bad weather, and simple changes of plan. The pilot, Jason Dahl, who had learned to fly before he could drive, rescheduled to get home to Colorado early so he and his wife could fly to London for their anniversary.

Among the passengers and crew, authorities say, were four young men who had trained for months and perhaps years for this moment, learning how to fight in small spaces and fly jets, lifting weights, and reciting prayers.

They all sat on the plane, delayed by the airport's heavy morning traffic, as American Airlines Flight 11 and United Airlines Flight 175 left Boston. They sat there as American Airlines flight 77 left Washington.

At 8:42 a.m. Flight 93 took off, light with passengers, heavy with 11,000 gallons of jet fuel for its cross-country flight. Nicole Miller's boyfriend watched it leave from his own plane as it sat on the tarmac.

Six minutes later the north tower of the World Trade Center erupted in flames.

For the next 30 minutes, it appears, Flight 93 soared west across Pennsylvania as havoc erupted behind it. Flight attendants, passenger accounts suggest, poured coffee and served breakfast.

One of the attendants, CeeCee Ross Lyles, was at the beginning of her career. She had dreamed of being a flight attendant since she took her first plane trip at age six but had just realized her dream a year ago, after six years of working as a police officer. Another, Sandra Bradshaw, was thinking about leaving her job so she could stay home with her children.

At some point before the plane reached Cleveland, the hijackers took over the plane, armed with knives and the threat of a bomb.

Around 9:30 a.m. air traffic controllers in Cleveland heard someone in the cockpit say, "Hey, get out of here!" a source said. Then a voice, in what was described as a thick Arabic accent, was heard that appeared to be addressing passengers even though it was radioed to air traffic control.

"This is your captain," the man said. "There is a bomb on board. Remain in your seats. We are returning to the airport."

How the hijackers overpowered the pilots remains unclear. One passenger would report in a telephone call that two people lay on the floor in the first-class cabin, either injured or dead. They appeared to be the pilot and co-pilot, he said, relating information from a flight attendant. Another told a friend that two people's throats were slit but didn't identify them. A third saw only one injured.

At least five passengers and flight attendants described the hijackers in their calls in similar terms: three men, wearing red bandannas, one with some sort of box strapped around his waist that he claimed was a bomb. One passenger reported that two of the hijackers were in the cockpit and a third guarded passengers in first class from behind a curtain.

None of the callers mentioned a fourth hijacker, although the FBI has identified four men in connection with the hijacking.

Those men are Saeed Alghamdi, Ahmed Ibrahim A. Al Haznawi, Ahmed Alnami and Ziad Jarrah.

It may be that the people who made calls were unable to see the fourth hijacker. Some news reports have suggested one may have already gained access to the cockpit as a uniformed guest pilot sitting in the spare jump-seat. Or, some terrorism experts suggest, he may have played a role as a backup, perhaps remaining unidentified among the other passengers or hiding in the bathroom until he was needed.

A Justice Department spokeswoman said Friday that their "best information" shows that four were involved.

By 9:36 a.m. United Flight 93 had suddenly changed course, according to flight-path information provided by Flight Explorer, a firm that supplies real-time radar tracking data. The plane had made a U-turn and was headed back toward Washington.

In the cabin passengers frantically began making calls, 23 from the seat-back phones alone from 9:31 to 9:53 a.m. Others passed cell phones to people who had been strangers just minutes before.

Why so many people were able to make calls while apparently under guard by hijackers could be that, as one passenger reported, there was no hijacker among the passengers in coach.

Some of the telephone calls were short—no more than a few rushed words of fear or love.

Lauren Grandcolas, flying home to San Rafael, California, from her grandmother's funeral, left a message for her husband saying her flight had been hijacked but she was "comfortable, for now."

Linda Gronlund and Joe Deluca, on their way to San Francisco for a vacation together, took turns. She called her sister to say she would miss her. He called his father.

"The plane's been hijacked," he said. "I love you."

Andrew Garcia, an Air National Guard air traffic controller and plane buff, only managed to get out his wife's name, "Dorothy," before his phone went dead.

Other passengers, though, managed to conduct fairly lengthy, even repeated conversations during the plane's final minutes, constructing a jumbled puzzle of what was happening inside the Boeing 757.

Deena Burnett was feeding her three daughters breakfast and watching the news in horror when the telephone rang in her home in San Ramon, California.

"Are you OK?" she asked her husband, Tom, 38.

"No," he said. "I'm on the airplane and it's been hijacked."

He told his wife the hijackers had stabbed someone. He told her to call the authorities, and he hung up.

When he called back, she was on the line to the FBI. She told him about the World Trade Center, the first he knew of the attack. He paused. "Were they commercial airplanes?" he asked.

Deena Burnett didn't think so. Cargo or private planes, she said.

"Do you know anything else about the planes?"

"No," she said.

"Do you know who was involved?" Again, she said no.

He told her the man who was stabbed had died.

The hijackers are talking about running the plane into the ground, he said. Then he said he had to go.

His third call came about 9:41 a.m., shortly after a plane had hit the Pentagon. "OK," he said. "We're going to do something."

In his fourth and final call, just before 10 a.m., Burnett said he was sure the hijackers didn't have a bomb, that he thought they had only knives.

"There's a group of us who are going to do something," he repeated.

Deena Burnett thought about her years of training as a flight attendant. She was taught to appease hijackers, to meet their demands, to stay in the background. She told her husband to sit down. "Don't draw attention to yourself," she said.

She told him she loved him. She felt he thought he was coming home that night. This was simply a problem that he was going to solve, as he had solved many others.

As Burnett talked with his wife, three other men who may have joined him in whatever plans were being hatched made calls of their own.

Across the aisle in Seat 4D, Mark Bingham, 31, called his mother. He was so rattled that when Alice Hoglan got on the line, her son told her, "This is Mark Bingham."

His message was brief: The plane had been hijacked by three men and he loved her.

In the rear of the plane, Jeremy Glick, also 31, a sales manager for a Web site firm and former judo champion, called his wife from a seat-back phone. He described three Middle Eastern men brandishing knives and a red box.

His wife told him about the attacks at the World Trade Center. He tried to grasp the hijackers' plans—to blow up the plane or fly it into a target?

The passengers had taken a vote among themselves, he said. They had decided to try to take back the plane.

"I told him to go ahead and do it," Lyzbeth Glick said on *Good Morning America*. "I trusted his instincts, and I said, 'Do what you have to do.' I knew that I thought he could do it."

Todd Beamer, 32, an account manager for Oracle, called a stranger. He picked up a seat-back phone and hit "0," and at 9:45 a.m. he was connected first to a dispatcher for GTE Airfone and then to Lisa Jefferson, the operator's supervisor.

For 13 minutes Beamer told Jefferson everything he could, passing along information he gleaned himself and from a flight attendant. The passengers remained in their seats, she said he told her, and the flight attendants were forced to sit in the back of the plane.

He told her how much he loved his pregnant wife and two sons, and he asked her to call them. He asked her to recite the Lord's Prayer and 23rd Psalm with him.

Moments later, Beamer told Jefferson about the plan, that the passengers were going to run up the long, narrow aisle to the first-class cabin and attack the hijacker there.

"I'm going to have to go out on faith," Beamer said.

He turned to someone else, and he said, "Are you ready?" Then, in the last words Jefferson would hear from him, "OK. Let's roll."

Sandra Bradshaw, the flight attendant, also identified three hijackers when she called her husband in Greensboro, North Carolina. She had been moved to the back of the plane, she said, but she and other passengers had a plan. They were going to rush their captors; she was boiling water to throw on them.

Another passenger, Elizabeth Wainio, also apparently talked of a plan to rush the hijackers. In a call she made to her stepmother in Baltimore, using the cell phone lent to her by Lauren Grandcolas, she said, "I've got to go now, Mom, they're breaking into the cockpit," according to the mother of another passenger who said she spoke with family members about the call. Wainio's parents declined comment.

The accounts of these calls—if accurate—would indicate that at least four people were somehow plotting to attack the hijackers. If Beamer's report is accurate, they were seated in different sections of the plane, with Bingham and Burnett up front, while the others were in the back.

It may be there were separate plans to take the plane or that somehow, amid all the telephone calls, chaos, and fear, the passengers were able to communicate with each other.

If they did, they may have known they had another pilot among them, Donald Greene, chief executive officer of Safe Flight Instrument in New York. Greene, according to his family, knew anything and everything about airplanes.

At about 9:54 a.m. the plane started flying erratically. In Oak Brook, Illinois, Jefferson heard screams in the background.

Two minutes later the plane's flight plan changed. The destination airport was changed from San Francisco International to Ronald Reagan National Airport. Estimated time of arrival: 10:28 a.m.

At nearly the same moment, from the plane's bathroom, someone called 911, repeating that Flight 93 had been hijacked, that this was not a hoax.

Then Marion Britton called a longtime friend, Fred Fiumano, at his New York City auto shop.

Britton, crying, told him the plane was turning around. It was going to go down.

"Don't worry about it," Fiumano said, trying desperately to reassure her. "They're only taking you for a ride."

He heard yelling and screaming in the background, and then the phone went dead. He tried to call the cellular-phone number back, but no one answered.

A few of the passengers expected they would win the battle. Before Lyzbeth Glick turned over the phone to her father because she couldn't bear to listen anymore, her husband told her, "Hang on the line. I'll be back."

At 10:03 a.m. a black crater bloomed in the soft earth of a field 80 miles southeast of Pittsburgh.

The wife in California, the father-in-law in New York, and the operator in suburban Chicago still held onto their phones.

They held on, waiting and hoping in the silence.

Tribune reporters Douglas Holt, Naftali Bendavid and Dan Mihalopoulos contributed to this report. This article originally appeared in the September 30, 2001, issue of the *Chicago Tribune.*

Aftermath of a Tragedy

By Kymberli W. Brady
California, USA

On Tuesday, September 11, 2001, ironically the anniversary of the Camp David Accord, American Airlines Flight 11 departed from Boston en route to Los Angeles. However, it would never reach its destination as it crashed into the south tower of the World Trade Center shortly before 8:45 a.m. eastern time, the result of a hijacking and a deliberate attack on United States soil. Eighteen minutes later, United Airlines Flight 175 from Boston to Los Angeles would also meet the same fate as it crashed into the World Trade Center's north tower, causing catastrophic loss of life and ultimate chaos in New York City.

Witnesses looked on in horror as people jumped from the two 110-story buildings, among them a man and woman holding hands, some 80 floors to their death in an effort to escape the engulfing flames. As we watched television from the safety of our homes, the horror escalated as all of America, and the world, witnessed the collapse of the first, and then the second, tower leaving a cloud of black smoke and ash that buried most of Manhattan. The only recognizable image remaining in the foreground of the devastation that enveloped the New York City skyline was the Statue of Liberty as she stood in the harbor, a surreal, uneasy glimpse of a country under siege.

Within an hour of the second plane crashing into the World Trade Center, a third plane, American Airlines Flight 77 en route from Washington, Dulles, to Los Angeles flew directly and deliberately into the Pentagon, an icon of our National Defense system, sending the entire country into a heightened state of emergency.

Later we would find out that another plane that crashed in Pennsylvania was also hijacked, but evidently missed its intended target, now believed to be the White House. A 911 operator reported that a passenger on United Airlines Flight 93 from Newark to San Francisco had locked himself in the bathroom to make the cell phone call shortly before the plane hit the ground.

After the dust settled, four planes were down, with an estimated 266 passengers and crew aboard the flights. The loss of lives in the Pentagon and World Trade Center Buildings, including police, fire, and rescue crews trapped inside as they collapsed, may never be actually known. By the time the recovery is completed, some 6,000 people are expected to have perished in the attacks.*

The Twin Towers, which took seven years to build, had been destroyed in a matter of hours, leaving an entire society in shock. The precise and well-planned execution of these attacks that violated our freedom and way of life succeeded in completely eradicating the World Trade Center, rocking our financial markets, and bringing US air travel to an immediate halt. This is a day destined to go down in history as our generation's Pearl Harbor.

As the news of the attacks spread to the west coast, a domino effect generated international evacuation of embassies and nationwide closures of federal buildings, major skyscrapers, theme parks, and transportation systems, bringing our country to a virtual standstill.

Many of us sat in shock, glued to the scenes that were unfolding on the news, as though it were a bad movie—one that would end as we awoke to yet another normal, American day. But the nightmare continued, as the days ahead would yield even more devastation and a global reaction of genuine horror from nations around the world.

President Bush, in a patriotic and determined statement to the world announced, ''Freedom itself was attacked this morning and I assure you freedom will be defended. These terrorists can shake the foundations of our largest buildings, but they cannot shake our resolve." It is this resolve that will hold America together in unity during the coming months and years as her citizens band together during the healing process.

Clearly one of the greatest tragedies this country has ever faced, this will be a day, not unlike that of Pearl Harbor, the assassination of President John F. Kennedy, and the Oklahoma City bombing, where we will all remember precisely where we were, as September 11, 2001 will go down in infamy as the end of the age of innocence.

"We mutually pledge to each other our lives, our fortunes and our sacred honor."

– The last words of *The Declaration of Independence*

*This story was written on September 12, 2001. It was later reported that 2,823 people died in the World Trade Center attacks.

8:45

By Carma Haley Shoemaker
North Carolina, USA

In the morning, the sun rises and gives birth to a new day.
But not at 8:45.
In the morning, children make their way to bus stops and
schools across the nation,
In hopes of sharing dreams, sharing stories, sharing smiles and
laughs.
But not at 8:45.
Each morning is a chance to start over,
To make this day even better then the last,
And to set a limit only to be broken by the day yet to come.
But not at 8:45.
Mornings should not be a time for terror.
Mornings should not be a time for fear.
Mornings should not be a time for pain and anguish.
Mornings should not be a time for sadness as those you love
are taken away,
Struck down in or at the prime of their lives,
Senselessly.
But they were at 8:45.
Mornings will never be the same again.
They will be a little less bright.
They will have a little less laughter.
They will be a little harder to endure.
At 8:45.

But to honor those whose lives were lost,
We get up each morning.
We will return to work—with tears in our eyes.
We will roll up our sleeves—with an ache in our soul.
We will pick up the pieces—with a hole in our heart.
And we will never, ever forget—8:45.

In Search of a Hero

By Helen Kay Polaski
Michigan, USA

I frowned, eased my chair back and drew a deep breath, and then—for the fourth time—erased the last two lines.

Nope. Sounded too much like a moron.

I expelled my breath slowly and let my fingers tip-toe across the keys again, this time trying to envision a sexy man...a sensitive man...a man who would make every woman's heart beat fast. What kind of man was a hero anyway?

Brrrinnnngggg!

Would my hero be the silent strong type?

Brrrinnnngggg!

Not afraid to let others see what he's made of...or what he believes in...someone who would give of himself for others.

Brrrinnnngggg!

Maybe a little rough around the edges...but with a sensitivity that should carry every woman from page one through to page 400. That would be the perfect romance hero! I grinned, ignoring the phone, then remembered my 16-year-old son was upstairs nursing a bellyache and quickly yanked the receiver off the hook.

"Hello."

"Do you have the TV on?" My neighbor asked, an urgency in her voice that made me forget about finding the perfect hero and move toward the TV room.

"No, why, is something wrong?"

"A plane crashed into one of New York's twin towers!"

My eyes scanned the room in search of the remote control. "You're kidding," I mumbled, sliding into my husband's easy chair and flipping on the set. "What happened? Did the pilot have a heart attack or something?"

"I don't know, but it's all over the news," she answered. "I think it's some terrorist bombing."

As the TV came to life, I got my answer. "Oh, my God. An airplane doesn't just fly into a building like that…" For a moment we remained silent, then we both spoke at once. Within a couple seconds, I had hung up the phone and called to my son. I didn't want him to see this by himself, nor did I want to watch it alone.

I went upstairs and sat on the edge of his bed. In silence we watched a second plane crash into the second tower. My son's eyes were wide and my hands began to shake. I knew the question in his mind was the same as in mine. *How could this happen in our country? This was no accident. Why hadn't someone stopped them?*

The TV reporters were going nuts trying to get all the information to the people as soon as they could, and my mind kept going back to the people in the towers. *What must they think? Did they know a plane had crashed into the towers? Did they feel a tremor when it happened? Were they in any danger? Would the explosions cause any other damage?*

One reporter said the people were being told they could leave but didn't have to, yet another reporter said they were being evacuated.

Good! Get them out, I thought, and wondered where my daughters and husband were and whether they knew this horrible thing had happened. I turned and locked gazes with my son, glad he was here with me and not witnessing this in school. Of a certainty, lives would be lost today.

We watched the emergency crews step up the job and keep the people moving. Reporters and news anchors relayed the information to us via the tube as we clutched the blankets and held our breath wondering what would happen next. *Would there be bombs? Would the people be safe once they got out of the building? A third plane? Oh, God, was this war? Biological warfare? Were deadly germs spreading across New York as we watched?*

Though our minds were filled with questions, we said very little out loud. Instead, we sat and watched, mesmerized by what was unfolding before our eyes. And then a reporter's voice, raised in disbelief, snapped us out of our stupor. The first tower had trembled. Shaken to its very core by the attack, it began to crumble into itself.

I gripped my hands together and physically recoiled from the TV. There were people in that tower! Oh dear God, they hadn't all gotten out—they couldn't have. But no, a reporter said they had…and then a puff of smoke and collectively we shook our heads in denial as the second tower shook itself into dust. No. They had not all gotten out.

Shocked and numb, we watched, unable to tear our eyes away. And the scene was replayed and replayed and replayed on every channel, etched in our memories forever.

Later that evening, I returned to my computer and, without a moment's hesitation, finished my description of a hero. He is silent; he is loud; he is funny. He is a father, a brother, a son. He is tall, short, and medium in height. He has eyes of every color and he wears rescue gear.

On the Beach

By M.J. Rose
Connecticut, USA

Tod's Point, Greenwich, CT—September 11, 2001—When you are jogging in this 147-acre park, there is a spot you pass at the halfway mark when you come around a bend, and on a clear day—like today—you can see the whole gleaming skyline of Manhattan.

Except this morning, there was something that seemed wrong.

There were two smokestacks on the horizon in a place there never had been smokestacks before. And it took a minute—a long minute—to figure out that the smoke was billowing out from the World Trade Towers.

About 20 yards up ahead, a few people had congregated, and I stopped to ask what had happened.

Their news was swift and delivered in short sentences.

At that point in time, both towers were still standing. And so we stood. All strangers gathered on an outcropping of rock, watching a scene that did not make sense.

And then a woman ran up and began to climb those rocks. She was crying and her movements were frantic. She could not get close enough to their edge—to the water. She was in tears. A few steps behind her another woman followed who tried to keep the first from climbing down the rocks to the water.

"But he's in that building," the crying woman said as she fought off her friend.

The crowd grew as the minutes passed. And some of us stood back to let the war widows past—you could tell who they were—the women and men who came—some alone, others with friends—who had loved ones in those two towers.

Ashamed to watch their grief, to see their trembling hands and smell their fear, I kept my eyes on the sky.

"It's collapsing," a man shrieked. And the wailing started.

In this suburb that sits on the outskirts of New York, we watched the Twin Towers fall. But we didn't hear the sirens or the explosions. We only heard the gulls screaming and the widows weeping.

Postscript—Five days later:

Every morning this week I have gotten into my car to go walking. I say I am not going back to Tod's Point—that I am going to the park where I cannot see the skyline—but I do go back. I have to go back and look again at the New York skyline.

The gaping hole is now as much a presence as the two towers once were, and the phrase "a negative space" has never had as much meaning for me.

Just as I have to keep sending money to the Red Cross and I have to keep crying, I have to keep looking at that negative space.

And so I will go back every day to stand, look, and for a moment honor all those people. The ones who are missing, the ones who worked the rescue, and the ones still living who will lose their lives some other day over what has been wrought.

The Events Leading to War

By Kyle Looby
Illinois, USA

A plane crash,
A building falls,
The phone rings,
A dreaded call.

A husband calls,
From tower one,
"Remember I love you;
Please kiss our son."

People running,
Panic ensues,
The cloud of debris,
Makes them all the same hue.

A brother aboard
The second plane;
A priest prays
While terror reigns.

A friend lost,
A cousin dead;
So many families
Wait in dread.
Disbelief and sorrow,

Anger abound.
So many lost,
Too few found.

A rush to judgment,
Anger brews.
A Muslim chased,
Though she's American, too.

A nation in mourning
For those who fell.
Candlelight vigils,
Churches ring the death knell.

America decides,
"We'll take no more.
One act of hatred,
And we're at war."

The Day the Planes Quit Flying

By Raynette Eitel
Nevada, USA

The day the planes quit flying over America,
An empty sky was filled with flames,
With mournful clouds
Weeping shrapnel and ash,
Burying innocence.

The day the planes quit flying over America,
Evil Davids tossed missiles
At twin Goliaths
And the world watched their fall.

The day the planes quit flying over America,
Grief rolled down the streets
In a ball of fire,
In a stream of smoke
Eclipsing the sun.
The day was dark,
The nightmare real.

The day the planes quit flying over America,
We watched the Pentagon,
That proud eagle,
Bleeding flames from its open wound.
Then that brave bird raised his head
Ready to fly
Like a phoenix rising from ashes.
He moved swiftly,
Eyes wary, searching,
Finding creatures hiding under rocks.

The day the planes quit flying over America,
Goodness began surpassing evil,
Lives laid down for others,
Heroes staring down unmitigated malice,
Flags filling empty spaces,
Candles lighted in dark places,
Love wrapping itself,
Cocoon-like around devastation.

And the world watching had no doubt
That butterflies
Would emerge one day,
The day the planes quit flying over America.

Two Thousand One, Nine Eleven

By Paul Spreadbury
Maine, USA

Two thousand one, nine eleven
Three thousand plus arrive in heaven.
As they pass through the gate,
Thousands more appear in wait.

A bearded man with stovepipe hat
Steps forward saying, "Let's sit, let's chat."
They settle down in seats of clouds,
A man named Martin shouts out proud,
"I have a dream!" and once he did.
The Newcomer said, "Your dream still lives."

Groups of soldiers in blue and gray,
Others in khaki, and green then say,
"We're from Bull Run, Yorktown, the Maine,"
The Newcomer said, "You died not in vain."

From a man on sticks one could hear,
"The only thing we have to fear."
The Newcomer said, "We know the rest,
Trust us sir, we've passed that test."

"Courage doesn't hide in caves.
You can't bury freedom, in a grave."
The Newcomer had heard this voice before—
A distinct Yankee's twang from Hyannisport shores.

A silence fell within the mist.
Somehow the Newcomer knew that this
Meant time had come for her to say
What was in the hearts of the three thousand plus that day.

"Back on Earth, we wrote reports,
Watched our children play in sports.
Worked our gardens, sang our songs,
Went to church and clipped coupons.
We smiled, we laughed, we cried, we fought—
Unlike you, great we're not"

The tall man in the stovepipe hat
Stood and said, "Don't talk like that!
Look at your country, look and see.
You died for freedom, just like me."
Then before them all appeared a scene,
Of rubbled streets and twisted beams—
Death, destruction, smoke, and dust,
And people working just 'cause they must—
Hauling ash, lifting stones,
Knee deep in hell, but not alone

"Look! Blackman, Whiteman, Brownman, Yellowman—
Side by side helping their fellow man!"
So said Martin, as he watched the scene
"Even from nightmares, can be born a dream."
Down below three firemen raised
The colors high into ashen haze.

The soldiers above had seen it before
On Iwo Jima back in '44.

The man on sticks studied everything closely,
Then shared his perceptions on what he saw mostly,
"I see pain, I see tears,
I see sorrow—but I don't see fear."

"You left behind husbands and wives,
Daughters and sons, and so many lives
Are suffering now because of this wrong.
But look very closely. You're not really gone.
All of those people, even those who've never met you,
All of their lives, they'll never forget you—
Don't you see what has happened?
Don't you see what you've done?
You've brought them together, together as one."

With that the man in the stovepipe hat said,
"Take my hand," and from there he led
Three thousand plus heroes, Newcomers to heaven
On this day, two thousand one, nine eleven.

Our Darkest Day

By Jolene Coiner
Oklahoma, USA

Somewhere today a child cries
For a mother who'll never come home.
A wife waiting to hear from her mate
Sits shaking by the phone.

A sister thinks about words she said
And knows she can't take back.
A brother screams out 'Why us, God?'
As dust settles from the attack.

In streets usually alive with bustle
Now silence and sirens are all that's heard.
Families looking for signs of hope
Just waiting for a word.

In the shadows of a tragedy
A nation is mourning from sea to sea.
Who could have done such an awful thing?
God, who can this demon be?

So many questions left unanswered,
So much pain left to be felt.
But as a nation we swear to our dead,
That justice will be dealt.

For they may have struck a horrible blow,
But they failed to remember one thing.
That even on our Darkest Day,
The bells of Liberty ring.

Footnote from the author:

Yesterday I just sat in stunned silence watching the TV and I admit a part of my mind kept saying, "This is just a bad dream, this is too much like a movie," but I knew that it wasn't.

We have lost so many due to an act of nothing short of pure cowardice. There is no justice in killing thousands of innocent people, but there will be justice in the end.

For all those who lost friends, family, and colleagues, I offer my deepest sympathies. Nothing can ever replace those you've lost. Only you know the depth of your pain.

As I said in this poem, those who attacked the U.S. either didn't know or just simply forgot that you can attack us, you can knock us down, and you can even cripple us, but you will never stop the bells of Liberty from ringing. You will never crush our spirit. You will never know the honor in being an American.

To my fellow Americans, I am immensely proud of you today.

Blessings to All,
Jolene Coiner

Lessons Learned On Tuesday

By Mary Dixon Lebeau
New Jersey, USA

Apparently there are stages to the plumage of smoke coming from a fire.

When a fire is at its most destructive, the smoke is black—strong, dark clouds of consumption filling the sky and thwarting any attempt to control it.

Later, as firefighters do their selfless jobs and try to contain the blaze, the smoke lightens to gray, indicating that some water has been added to it. Later still, the plumage turns white. By that point, the firefighters have made great strides towards extinguishing the fire and ending its destruction.

That's one thing I learned on Tuesday.

In all honesty, though, I'm not sure that it's true. It was just one idea—one theory thrown out by a newscaster as he watched the black cloud of smoke rising from what was once the symbol of financial activity, the World Trade Center. We were all throwing out ideas by that time, trying in that way humans do to explain the unexplainable, to put words to our terror and anger and grief.

Silly humans—like any words can explain what happened to us on Tuesday. Explanations seem impossible. The best we can do is to recount what we learn and hold onto what we have left.

So this is what I learned: our security, our freedom—our lives, really—are very precious and equally as fragile. Since

Tuesday, we've been hearing the stories, the voices of people who fought for their lives and for our freedom. Some are stories of bravery, like the story of the firefighters who rushed to the World Trade Center to handle the disaster, only to lose their own lives when the massive building crumbled and fell.

Other stories are heartbreaking, like the pair of financial workers who held hands and leapt from the World Trade Center, falling to certain death while trying to escape the horror that enveloped that building.

Thanks to the media, we all have these images. What we don't have—not yet—is a method to deal with the horror. I watched the doomed rogue plane tear into the skyscraper, and all I could think of was the terror that those poor travelers felt as they realized what was happening. A plane full of people—sons and fathers, grandmothers, and friends—crashes and explodes. Families are shattered, blown up along with the New York skyline.

It's unimaginable. Someone wake me quickly, before I see too much and I'm unable to forget this nightmare.

We can't forget. America, for all her wisdom, grew up a bit on Tuesday. Never again will we feel as safe—heck, we were downright smug—walking down a city street, visiting our nation's capital, hopping a cross-country plane to visit family or take care of business. Our innocence fell with the sky towers and collapsed like the Pentagon building. We feel hurt and vulnerable, equal parts angry and afraid.

I want to do something—anything—to make this go away. But I have no answers.

"Can we move, mom?" my 11-year-old asked when he reached me by phone as the events were playing out on Tuesday.

"Why, Steven?" I asked him, wanting to know what he knew, to learn how scared he had become since I sent him to the bus stop that morning.

"We're stuck here between the biggest city, New York, and the most important city, Washington," he explained, telling me what I already thought myself as I watched the east coast being attacked that morning. "This isn't really a safe place to be."

"Where would you go?" I asked aloud, while my heart prayed, *Please, where can I keep you safe?*

"Mississippi, I guess, or Ohio," he ventured, and I agreed to think about it.

But we aren't safe anywhere, really. We will always be looking over our shoulder, double-checking the stranger across the way. Never again will we take our safety for granted. Our eyes have been opened; our lives as changed as the skyline that turned to ashes and smoke. This is something else I learned on Tuesday.

What I didn't learn is what to do with all this. So I do the only thing I know how—I pray. I pray that our leaders make wise decisions. I pray that we keep our heads but stay true to our hearts. I pray most of all that this is all over—soon—and that we don't have to pay dearly for the justice we rightfully seek.

I pray that God continues to bless America.

Tuesday night, after hours of watching the news, I went upstairs to check on my youngest son. "I'm watching Scooby Doo," Max told me. I joined him on the bed, studying his sweet face as he stared intently at his world of mysterious machines and Scooby snacks, where problems were solved in 23 minutes and every ending was happy.

And I prayed that, for a while, our children could keep believing that. I closed my eyes and tried to imagine what life will be like after the white smoke clears.

Destination: Heaven

By Shannon Leigh
North Carolina, USA

Morning was breaking just outside L.A.
Daddy was supposed to be comin' home today.
But he's gonna miss her bedtime,
No story will be read.
For the very first time…she's gonna tuck herself into bed.

He was getting married in Boston next May;
Just flew into town to see his fiancée.
She wished she said she loved him,
Just one last time.
She can't believe…he really meant good-bye.

If your heart is breaking,
You're not alone.
You can hear tears falling
All around the globe.
For those who flew United and American...
Destination: Heaven.

Her parents married in 1945.
They were in New York City just to see the sights.
Mom was in a wheelchair,
Dad was by her side.
To think of them dying like that…makes her cry.

He served our country for 30-odd years.
Workin' in the Pentagon to alleviate our fears.
And for what?
Did he die in vain?
Things aren't ever going to be the same...

If your heart is breaking,
You're not alone.
You can hear tears falling
All around the globe.
For those up to Floor 111...
Destination: Heaven.

They're going home—they're going home.

If your heart is breaking,
You're not alone.
You can hear tears falling
All around the globe.
For those on Flights 175 and 11...
For those who flew 93 and 77...
For those who died while trying to help on 9/11...

Destination: Heaven

The Day the World Fell Off its Axis

By Alaine Benard
Louisiana, USA

❝The U.S.—Under Attack!"

"Oh, I'm watching the Trade Center burning across the river from where I sit at my desk…No one can get through to relatives over there. Oh! Never in my life has anything hit me this hard. I want to go home…I'm so sick. Help us all, Jesus."

"Planes destroying New York Trade Towers, Camp David hit! All airports closed. War imminent!"

"Dear God—has anyone heard from Teri-Bean and Annie? They're in New York and Washington. *Pray!* Everyone pray for them and this nation..."

"This is the worse day in the history of the US! My 22-year-old son is in the military, and I can't get through to him! What am I going to do? What's going to happen?"

"Los Angeles elementary school incinerated? Does anyone have information on that? *God!* Is this the end of the world?!"

"Please, please pray for our leaders, pray for all the hurt, dying, and trapped souls! Send your army, Lord! Protect us and help the emergency workers in this hour of need!"

"10,000 known dead in New York…"

"My son-in-law flies the new Army helicopters and no one can find him! His wife and two small kids are hysterical. No information! Send word if anyone online hears anything!"

***

Amid unopened birthday presents and cards, I sit staring at the September 11 nightmare screaming across my monitor. As an artist, graphics burn permanent images into my mind. Therefore, I am unable to turn on the television or read the explicit details...until later. When I digest the horrors that take root and become real, I may be able to see them.

Dizziness and sweat make me lay my head on my keyboard as I battle to regain control. Is my heartbeat causing this nausea, or has the earth finally left its axis to spin all its inhabitants crazily into space?

My first thoughts are from the "me" that is a mother. I want to retrieve my son from school, mere blocks from the city's largest refinery, Exxon. Getting news that all non-emergency plant employees have been sent home adds impetus to my overwhelming need to protect my son. The school will not release the children, in an attempt to quell the panic sweeping the city. Baton Rougeans are well aware that we are known as "Refinery Alley" and are a major hit target for terrorists. Confirmed reports tell that President Bush has landed at Barksdale Air Force Base, in nearby Shreveport. I leave my son, my relatives, and the entire nation—blanketed in prayer. All calls are those asking for prayer, and I gladly answer because it comforts me and allows me to take some action. This beats back the runaway Mom emotions that are keeping me feeling panicky.

My head speaks next—the "me" that is rational and calm under pressure. Realistically my options for actions are limited. I can pray and trust—nothing more. Therefore, the brunt of my emotional force focuses on the US government and military. Yearning for torpedoes-be-damned leadership, I fervently wish for take-charge men like Macarthur, Churchill, Patton, and Roosevelt. America has lost much honor, strength, and respect with the error-ridden campaigns of Vietnam, Bosnia, Desert Storm, and other "conflicts" not handled in the great American tradition of bygone eras.

The estimated death tolls from today are already surpassing previous war totals. What possible conclusion is there other than a declaration of war? This is my gut talking. War. Chilling thoughts overtaken by the thankfulness that my own child is not old enough to be called to military duty. My heart goes out to the mothers of older sons. How do they endure the terror they feel?

Listening to radio interviews with ex-secretary of state, Hague, the war seems steps closer. John McCain's impassioned speeches promoting aggressive action and retribution resemble pre-war speeches of the past. Pearl Harbor is being mentioned more as the day wears on. What seemed impossible hours ago now twists my insides with the mounting probability.

As we await the nation's next move, a prevailing sense of sadness descends. Looking at my son, eyes closed in prayer for the thousands murdered today, I wonder how September 11, 2001, will affect his childhood memories. I recall my own experiences with second graders gathering around a tiny black and white TV to watch the first man walk on the moon. I remember watching my Vietnam POW walk across the tarmac of home as I twirled the ID bracelet around my wrist. I visualize the exact place in time when I heard the news that John F. Kennedy had been assassinated and when Martin Luther King met the same fate.

Of all the feelings experienced today, shock is conspicuously absent. Grief, worry, physical symptoms, relief, and worry, yes. Not one soul I encountered today expressed the slightest bit of disbelief, leaving me to wonder when this once-great nation become so cynical. Perhaps we will feel the shock in the days to come. How did we come to accept terrorism to the degree that when our own orbit changes course, we aren't struck down with disbelief?

On the positive note, each and every conversation I joined in, read about, or listened to, included moments of prayer. From local people to friends and connections across the world, each person added their own intentions to the great circle of worship formed today.

The world needs powerhouse leadership and prayer to get back on track. Will it take a war to put God back in His rightful place in the home, the schools, and in government? We can hope that the fallacies of political correctness will soon be replaced by doing what is right in the sight of God and in our own heart. Maybe then, all will be put right in our universe.

You Rushed In

By Dari Lavender
Georgia, USA

I wonder who you are, you who raced to the World Trade Center. Why did you fight the surging crowds to go inside a building others prayed to exit?

What gene did you possess that enabled you to hurry to possible death while thousands of your fellow Americans fought to escape that same fate?

How can mere training account for men and women racing up stairs toward a raging inferno thousands of feet in the sky, all the while understanding that they may have to keep right on going, past the inferno, past the highest floor, on to eternity?

Who are you?

And you, down there on the street—what caused you to stay there, willing the throngs of humanity away from the very spot you stand, below a building angrily spitting balls of fire in all directions?

Why didn't you leave when you had the chance? How can duty to a job account for such determination to save lives, knowing that it may cost you yours?

Who are you?

What about you—who had no job duties, no training? You who we may never know about—you who stopped to help your fallen comrades, not knowing what that act might cost you?

You took charge in the midst of chaos, calling out to stay calm, and hurry toward the exits. You turned back at the last minute to help someone slow, hysterical, or injured.

You stopped in your wild race for freedom to help the helpless who had fallen, unable to make it without you.

Who are you, who rushed to your death—you who stood your post while death rained down on you from the sky, you who might have made it out but chose to slow your own progress to speed someone else's?

You are firefighters, police officers, and average citizens. No amount of training, duty, or responsibility enabled you to do what you did. It was in your spirit, your genes, your very DNA, to make the ultimate sacrifice on September 11, 2001.

They say that fools rush in where angels fear to tread. There were no fools there that day. There were only heroes, and we will not forget what you did.

No More Days

By Shirley Ann Walker Young
Georgia, USA

I could feel the tightness of the air.
There was heartache and tears everywhere.
The rescue efforts were in vain
as yet, there was another plane.
A mother cries,
A father screams.
Destroyed are so many dreams.
Given warning—there was none.
Mothers and fathers lost their sons.
Daughters were taken,
Daddies were, too.
Oh, what torment it put us through.
A child without a mothers love,
without a single one last hug.
The air is thick,
Our hearts are heavy.
Tears are falling
for there are
no more days
to laugh, to sing.
Our heads are bowed over America
and hearts are heavy, too,
for our friends both young and old
have been taken on this day—

September 11,
And for them there
are no more days!

Not Just Another Morning

By Margaret Helmstetter
Arizona, USA

Just another morning—
Make the coffee,
Open the eyes,
Turn the TV on.
News just starting—
First cup.
Brain starting,
Anchor talking,
A movie preview.
No!
It's real.
NO, NO, NO!
Crying.
Hurting.
Wondering *why?*
Wondering *how?*
The beauty destroyed,
The lives taken.
No sense.
No reason why.
Strength rising

from the ashes.
News coming in
of safety found.
A world cries,
A mother mourns.
A new source
Of strength is found.

2

United We Stand

"This is a day when all Americans, from every walk of life, unite in our resolve for justice and peace. America has stood down enemies before, and we will do so this time."

— President George W. Bush
September 11, 2001

Simply Americans

By Victoria Walker
Florida, USA

Evil is trying to destroy America. He has her in his grasp; he has inflicted harm upon her heart and spilled her blood upon her own soil. But America will never allow evil to prevail. Evil can bomb her buildings, steal innocent lives, and even wound her spirit, but he can never defeat her. For America is a strong nation, built by men and women from all corners of the world who were willing to give their lives for liberty.

Over the past two centuries, a countless number of men and women—who proudly declared themselves Americans—have died so that you and I would be guaranteed *Life, Liberty and the pursuit of Happiness.* We cannot allow their sacrifices to be for naught; we cannot succumb to evil's threats—we cannot allow evil to win.

Evil watches with glee as America's people bicker and fight amongst themselves. He may think that our internal feuds make us weak—that our differences will tear us apart. He is wrong. Americans are strong, they are steadfast, and they are brave. There is a saying, "When the going gets tough, the tough get going!" Today, times are tough here in America, but America will endure the difficulties thrown her way, and she will triumph—of this, I have no doubt.

America and everything she stands for is being attacked by the flames of evil. But when the smoke clears, America and her people will still be standing with their heads held high. The torch of liberty will still be shining proudly for the world to see; the stars and stripes will still be waving bravely in the breeze; and America's people will still be standing side by side—rebuilding her damaged structures with the courage and bravery that has made her the greatest country on this earth.

Today, we are no longer black or white Americans, Native Americans, Hispanic Americans, or Asian Americans—we are all bound together by one common thread. We are all simply—*Americans*. As Americans, we must stand together, for if we do not, we will surely fall together. We can no longer allow ourselves to judge our neighbor by the color of his skin, the church he attends, the clothing he wears, or the language he speaks. To hate your neighbor for his differences is exactly what evil is hoping for, for evil thrives on hatred. By inflicting hatred and prejudice, you will become the very evil that threatens to destroy our great nation. Though evil does not know it, our differences are what make us strong—our different views allow us to see from many angles, our different languages allow us to communicate globally, and our different religions teach us all to love each other…and to hope; *hope for the future, hope for peace, hope for America, hope for the world.*

Freedom In America

By Shelle Castles
Mississippi, USA

September 11, 2001, will live in epiphany for all of us. I'm sure each one of us can remember exactly what we were doing, where we were headed, and even what plans we were making when we heard or saw or read about the events unfolding before our very eyes early that Tuesday morning.

Our life as we remember it is no longer the same. Each one of us has been deeply touched and deeply affected by what has happened.

We stare in shock at the mass destruction. We cry tears of anger and frustration. We mourn the loss of immeasurable lives.

And yet, the terrorist attacks on our country and its people have been in vain.

We pull together in times of need to carry on. We cry tears of pride and joy at the countless miracles and the love of a nation that stands strong and proud. We are a people, uniquely different and yet—the same.

Because we live in freedom.

It is the love of our nation that bonds us in strength. It is the love of our people that carries us through national crisis. It is the love of our freedom that has prepared us to fight.

As the weeks continue, as the months go by, our lives will be ever changing. We will suffer even more and we will mourn even harder. The unknown future is sure to affect our lives each day.

As we struggle through these trying times, still counting on those miracles, still prayerfully asking God to keep His mighty hand on us and our loved ones, remember this: we are America.

We are America who has fought for her freedom. We are America who struggled through growing pains, developing a democracy and building up cities. We are America who gives unselfishly to those in need. We are America who has never been crushed. We are America who will never give up.

God Bless this America and its people. God Bless this America and those who lost their lives so tragically. God Bless this America and those who unselfishly give up their time and resources to help. God Bless this America and the government who maintains our freedom. God Bless this America and those who fight for our freedom. God Bless this America and those who make it America.

United We Stand

By Teraisa J. Goldman
Nevada, USA

Undescribable.
That's what you are.
Terrorist action out of manic nation.
Not just stone or steel.
Or bodies broken.
Hearts forever cracked.
You came like the thief.
We were forewarned.
But busy in life.
Together we now stand.
You are alone.
And against the world.

Gray

By Mary E. Tyler
Virginia, USA

When we focus on our differences,
we see yellow, black, red, white.
When we walked uptown on the highway,
we were all the color of concrete dust.

You Are My Neighbour...

By Heather O'Neil
Ontario, Canada

You are my neighbour.
Until this moment, I took you for granted.
You were always there, sitting quietly.

Occasionally I visited you.
Admired your strength and your beauty.
Bought your wares and ate your food.

You are my neighbour.
Until today, I presumed you would always be okay.
You were bigger than life...invincible.

I watched your progress from afar.
Wondered at your eloquence in distant lands.
Watched your development with wonder.

You are my neighbour.
Today I realized my life is forever twined in yours.
That I depend upon you for my life.

That without you, I may not be free...
That without you, I may not live in peace...
That without you, I am vulnerable.

You are my neighbour.
Today I cried for you, felt your pain and anger.
Watched horrified at the wounds inflicted upon you.

Today I also watched you rise.
Victorious from the ashes, strong and firm.
United against the enemy without.

You are not my neighbour,
You are my friend, my confidante, my ally,
You have the strength that keeps me strong.

You are my friend.
We may not always agree, see eye to eye…
But we stand beside each other united when it really matters.

Friend, neighbour, ally…
America, we feel your pain, your sorrow,
And like a good friend, we are here, to lean on should you need us.
God Bless America, today, tomorrow and always…friends.

No Longer Afraid

By Kathryn Lay
Texas, USA

Even as my daughter and I sat mesmerized by the events of September 11, I wondered how this would affect the English as a Second Language school my husband and I directed for local refugees and immigrants. So many of our students were Muslim.

Would they come back? Would our volunteer workers feel comfortable with the students? Would my daughter or I?

For days, we mourned over the loss of life and security in our country. My husband and I talked about what we should do about our students. Finally he sat down and began calling our students who came from around the world, running from their own wars and hate to find happiness and a future for their families here in America.

"Oh, I am so afraid. I do not leave my apartment," one of the women told us.

"People stare at us," another said.

A father who is of Arab background told how his son was harassed in school.

Richard assured them we loved them and were their friends.

One woman who had previously volunteered to help babysit our students' children during classes told us, "I will not go there with Muslims."

My heart hurt. These people were our friends. They grieved over the horrors of September 11. They loved America. They were afraid.

The first night of classes, only our Asian and Hispanic students came to class. The next week our van drivers called some of the women. One agreed to come.

At the church my husband greeted her. She clasped his hand and quietly said, "I have gone no where. But here, I can come. I know I am safe."

Many of our students had had that same sentiment when they'd first arrived in America. But now, they were afraid.

By the next week, a vanload of Muslim women and children arrived to work on their English skills. Many were new students. Word had gotten around that we loved them; we were there to help. And, they weren't afraid.

Soon after, I drove down the road near our home. The American flag could be seen flying from atop mailboxes, homes, and on the antennas of cars.

I saw a little boy standing in his front yard. I didn't know what country he was from originally. I didn't know his religion, his family beliefs, or his background. I didn't know what language he spoke in his home.

He had a small flag and waved it back and forth, back and forth. I slowed down and waved. He waved the flag at me and smiled.

Where was he from? Did it matter? He was here. He was proud of his new home. As were my ancestors who arrived long ago. They were probably afraid at times. Sometimes, I am, too.

But I am also proud. Proud to live in America. And because of that, I am proud that my family and I have the chance to love and help those who are strangers.

To my daughter, they are not strangers. They are new friends waiting to be made. God bless America. And God bless the children who play with their friends, unafraid, ride their bi-cycles, unafraid, and wave the flag, unafraid.

It's time for me to let go of fear and wave a few flags.

Noble Eagle

By Julie Weed Brendel
Indiana, USA

The Red, White and Blue stand Mighty and Proud,
and shall rise above this Big Black Cloud.
For when people are weak and life seems so bleak,
we mourn from our sorrow and our grief.
From out of the ashes the "NOBLE EAGLE" shall rise,
look out bin Laden it's about your demise!
For you sent men and boys to do your Dirty Deed,
not for your "ALLAH" but your cowardly greed.
You thought your strikes would conquer and divide,
so you bin Laden should run and should hide.
For the wrath of the "Noble Eagle" will soar in the sky
and hunt you down until the day you die.
You thought we would crumble, but you were so wrong,
for now the USA and all nations stand strong!

A Lesson in Acceptance of Diversity

By Catherine C. Harris
North Carolina, USA

Last night, I sat down with my three children and let them talk about their fears. All three children had a common question: "Why?" That question is on the lips of people worldwide. As we ask the universe, "why?" we are also asking other important questions: What can we learn from this? What can we tell our children? Is there a life lesson here?

The life lesson may be one that we've tried to promote in the last several decades. That acceptance of diversity (sexual, religious, size, color, ethnic, etc.) is not a cutesy cause—that it is a serious and very important mission.

I was able to take my children to www.Positive PerfectYou.com and show them that we are doing something in an attempt to change things, so that people like the ones who committed these terrible acts wouldn't have a hate platform to stand on anymore. I told them that hate kills... sometimes on a small scale and sometimes on a scale so large that it changes the world forever.

Hate stands up to say that anyone "different" from us must be wrong or unnatural. Hate turns ordinary people into criminals, murderers, and voices against freedom. Hate is sometimes green with envy, and it is often deadly.

However, even when hate tries to destroy peace, courage, spirit, and love, it will always fail. Men and women gave their lives September 11, 2001, in an effort to save their fellow citizens; this is courage. Men and women stood on the capital steps and sang, "God bless America, the land that I love;" this is spirit. Men and women lined up by the hundreds to give their blood; this is love. Men, women, and children across the country cried together and prayed together; this is peace.

There is an important message here. We cannot allow hate to invade and destroy. Where there is acceptance of diversity, hate loses its stronghold on humanity. Talk to your children about the importance of accepting different ideas, opinions, and religious convictions. The only way to fight the cowardice of hate is with the courage of love.

Discrimination

By Shannon Roudebush
Indiana, USA

The hatred within
of dark hair and dark eyes,
Judging by skin
will bring our demise.

Not our fault, not theirs.
Who then to blame?
All the world shares
in USA shame.

Shame for blood shed
on our very own land.
Shame for the dead,
we should all lend a hand.

Working together,
the world can unite.
No question of whether
or not we will fight.

Light-skinned or dark,
hold a hand in yours.
From the very first spark,
no one wins wars.

Judging Leesa

By Michelle Pearson
Illinois, USA

Like millions of other Americans, Leesa Clark was horrified by the events of September 11.

From her home in New Jersey, Leesa grappled with all of the same emotions that so many others did. Why did this happen? Who would do such a horrible thing? Are we safe? Are our children safe? Will things ever be the same again?

A week after that horrible Tuesday, trying to return to some semblance of normalcy in their lives, Leesa and her husband, Kevin, made a trip to their local Target to pick up some things they needed. Upon their arrival, they went their separate ways with Leesa making her way to the back of the store where the pet food was located.

As she stood choosing dog food for the family pet, a man walked past her. He stared at her, then walked down an adjacent aisle. He came back past her and stared at her again.

By this time, Leesa began feeling uncomfortable. "He was staring at me as if he could see right through me," she says. She began wishing her husband were closer at hand.

The man stood and stared at her some more and then finally spoke.

"Go back to your country," he said. "Your kind aren't welcome in America anymore."

"I was totally shocked," says Leesa. "At first, I thought I had misheard him."

"Excuse me?" Leesa asked the man.

"You heard me," the man said with hate in his voice. "Get out of my country!"

Leesa stood and looked at the man, trying to comprehend what he was saying. She couldn't believe what she was hearing.

The ongoing tragedy of America after September 11 has been the small-mindedness and prejudice of some of its citizens.

A visit to the Web site of ABC News finds a chat board filled with talk of outlawing the Muslim faith and destroying the culture of Islam. I have even seen messages suggesting that Arab-Americans be interned the way Japanese-Americans were during WW II. What a shame that our country has come so far in so many ways, and yet there are those who continue to stereotype others.

I'm of German and Scotch-Irish descent. That doesn't make me a Nazi, nor does it make me fond of drinking. I'm a Christian. That doesn't make me an abortion clinic bomber.

Like the gossip that people so often love to indulge in by spreading lies and making absurd judgments based on nothing but rumor and without any basis in fact whatsoever, judging somebody by their skin color or religion or ethnic background is ludicrous. Condemning an entire people based on the actions of a few is insane.

Leesa Clark says she will use her experience with the man filled with hate to teach her children about tolerance and respect for people of all races and religions. Because when the man told Leesa to go back to her own country, he was basing his judgment on her brown skin and her long, black, braided hair.

You see, Leesa has more of a right to be here than most of us. And that's exactly what she told the man who suggested she didn't belong. He was now the one who was shocked, and he scurried off, mumbling an apology that Leesa could barely hear.

Leesa is a Wampanoag native, the tribe whose members helped the Pilgrims survive their first winter in the New World. Her ancestors' tribe, the Chappaquiddick, lived on Martha's Vineyard long before our ancestors arrived.

Let Leesa Clark's experience be a lesson. "Please be careful and don't let hatred blind you," she says. "You simply cannot judge a person by their looks. You also cannot judge a nation of people based on the actions of a few."

Patriotism Reborn

By Raynette Eitel
Nevada, USA

I never knew years of singing
About the sweet land of liberty
Was wedging love so securely
In my heart
That it might break.

I never dreamed humming
"God bless America"
Would become a daily prayer
To deliver my country
From evil.

I never suspected that
All those times I bellowed
"The Star Spangled Banner"
Just before the first pitch
Would one day be so
Filled with anger.

I have lived from sea to shining sea
Beside that purple mountain
Just above the fruited plain
In a country where I
Took freedom for granted,

Worshipped God as I chose,
Said whatever I pleased,
Bore arms when I wished,
Never truly grasping
My extraordinary birthright.

It is time now for remembering
What America is all about,
Songs still sung,
Hands held over broken hearts,
Flags waving proudly
From the New York harbor
To the redwood forest,
Tears streaming down our cheeks,
Thoughts of Bunker Hill
Gettysburg, Verdun, Pearl Harbor,
The 38th Parallel, Vietnam,
Twin Towers.

Now that I am reborn with tears
And smoke and fire
Into patriotism,
Drinking the milk of freedom,
Wrapped in the red, white, and blue
Of my old flag,
I sing new lullabies
Of the songs of my fathers
And vow to protect and defend
America the rest of my life.

Banners and Weapons

By Sharon M. Thompson Loomis
Wisconsin, USA

I casually sit on the side of the road,
waiting for the parade to start. I look
down the road and see all the excited people
who are as anxious as myself.
I hear the drum beats drawing nearer and nearer.
The sticks tap the drum as rain taps the
ground and fades into the surface of the earth.
I relax in my chair watching every music lover
pass by.
I clap as each group passes, and as
each one approaches. I picture myself
in the band receiving some attention,
but each drum beat startles me.

You watched me sit there and dream,
lost in my thoughts,
but you have upset me by interrupting.
You wanted peace, but it seems that you've
made war. You wanted the world to stop fighting,
so you broadcast with banners and made a lot of speeches.
You've stood in the way of the Army, Navy, Marines, and Air
Force bands.
I withdrew from my dream, shocked
at what was happening.

You could see warplanes in my eyes,
trying to shoot you down.
Then you were hit, taken away.

Who directed you my way?
Who assured you that you would get away with it?
Who commanded you to capture my happiness?
so that you could have some?
All I want is for you to stop and enjoy,
even though I won't stop enjoying
to help you destroy.
I remain seated among the crowd.
They are my friends, as I am theirs,
and I enjoy as they do.
I do not see fighter planes flying over,
nor any sign of war coming from
the President's mouth.

Seeing you, I imagine you free from protests,
enjoying the bands.
I imagine myself free
from protests,
and we sit together and enjoy
instead of destroying each other with
BANNERS and WEAPONS.

Standing Tall

By Kymberli W. Brady
California, USA

In this country we stand tall, a nation proud and free.
Now one day has changed it all, and soiled our liberty.

In horror we watched the towers fall, our terror burned inside.
After the fires came the rain, as if Heaven itself had cried.

Those behind this gruesome deed died as men of shame.
Now every single American will never be the same

But what they didn't know, in trying to change this land,
was that we would soon grow stronger—united we would stand.

And like our lady Liberty, who still stands tall and proud,
we see her flame still burning, and we call her name out loud.

Our nation's flag is proudly seen, waving everywhere.
Red, white, and blue reminds us of how we got her there.

In a show of love and faith, we'll hold our banners high.
And through the tears, we will rebuild. Again, we'll reach the sky.

The world sees us crying; they are crying too.
But we will soon be whole again, and we will rise anew.

They say what doesn't kill us makes us stronger, this is true.
For forever we'll stand proud, behind our red, white, and blue.

Rise Up, America!

By Garry E. Chartier
British Columbia, Canada

Rise up, great nation, take your stand,
Respect and dignity demand;
Defend the honor of your land,
America.

Though some your glorious heights have spurned,
And on your face their venom burned,
Your firm resolve they have not turned,
America

From out the ashes and the scars
We see on blue the gleaming stars,
The red and white of banner bars,
America.

Rise up! You've nothing now to dread,
With courage lift your dauntless head;
Take up the torch held by your dead,
America.

Hold fast! Let not your foes displace
Your rank within the human race,
For God has blessed you with his grace,
America.

Although the battle may be long,
You yet will sing the victor's song
And with the help of God keep strong,
America.

E'en though your enemies assail,
Take heart! Your efforts will not fail;
With trust in God you will prevail,
America.

3

American Reflections

"The attacks of September 11th were intended to break our spirit. Instead, we have emerged stronger and more unified. We feel renewed devotion to the principles of political, economic, and religious freedom, the rule of law and respect for human life. We are more determined than ever to live our lives in freedom."

— Rudolph W. Giuliani
Mayor of New York City
December 31, 2001

It Could Have Been Me

By Lori Williams
New York, USA

I was plowing the fields, sitting in a boardroom, teaching a child—yet I was there. I was selling insurance, ringing up purchases, patrolling the neighborhood—yet I was there. I was grooming a dog, serving lunch, recording a CD—yet I was there. I was there because I am an American, and it could have been my city. It could have been my husband, wife, son or daughter, mother or father. It could have been me. I feel your pain as if it was my own...and it is.

I remember seeing things on TV in places like Israel and Bosnia that made my heart ache, so I turned the channel. It was not my home. I remember thinking, *What if that happened here?* and brushing it off...never! This is America! Things like that don't happen here!

Well, they happened, and I am humbled by my ignorance. Today I will hug my children longer, tell my spouse how much he means to me, and go out into the fresh air to smell freedom. I will make the phone calls I've been putting off, thank my mom for raising me right, and smile at everyone I pass on the street. Today I will embrace life like never before!

I may not have been there next to you in New York, Washington, or Pennsylvania on September 11—I may have been in courtrooms, schoolrooms, or mailrooms, but I was there in spirit, as an American...as someone who realizes finally, exactly what that means.

The Reflection

By Alaine Benard
Louisiana, USA

Pearl Harbor bomb Bin Laden;
    the echo of revenge.
Dead soldiers raise their carbines
    for freedom now impinged.
Conscience screams "no eye for eye,"
    must turn the other cheek.
Justice, judgment, punishment;
    the Lord's alone to seek.
Thus the nation's looking glass
    reflects our own turmoil;
to walk the path of the Word
    or honor homeland soil.

I Remember

By Mary M. Alward
Ontario, Canada

I remember as a small child hearing my parents speak in hushed tones of war. They spoke quietly of Dad's brother, Uncle Bill, and how his life would be forever changed by the wounds he had sustained when he and his buddies of the Royal Hamilton Infantry, together with other Canadians and the English, landed at the Second Front—Dieppe.

I remember Uncle Bill showing us where pieces of shrapnel had entered and exited his body, leaving gleaming, white scars that would remain with him for the rest of his life.

When I was very young, I remember the sad look on my mother's face and the tears in her eyes when she heard the word, "Korea." I wondered how the mention of a place so far away could make my usually smiling mother turn her head and swipe away a tear.

I remember, too, as a small child being terrified of airplanes. If I heard the drone of a plane while playing in the yard of my southern Ontario home, I would run and hide in the corner where the chimney met the house. After all, planes meant bombs. Even though there had been no bombing on Canadian soil, I had heard the hushed whispers of family members speaking of "The Blitz" in England. And if I remember correctly, my brother had told me that planes brought bombs. Since he was not much older than I was, it is obvious that he didn't think it would leave me trembling every time I heard an approaching plane.

I remember going to school on November 11 (Remembrance Day in Canada) and standing at attention, silent tears welling when I thought of the men who had given their lives that I might live in a free country.

I remember Uncle Bert, who was stationed in Holland at the end of the war, and how thankful the people of that country were to the Canadian Liberators.

I remember as a teenager hearing the word "Vietnam" and wondering why there was no peace in the world. I remember, too, the draft dodgers who ran to Canada to avoid fighting for their country.

I remember November 23, 1963, when my teacher left the room to answer the phone and came back, tears streaming down her face, to announce that President John F. Kennedy of the United States had been assassinated in Dallas, Texas.

I remember working in a bar and seeing a Vietnam veteran, not much older than 20 years, come in still dressed in his camouflage.

I remember watching the footage of the assassinations of Martin Luther King, Jr., and Robert Kennedy.

I remember Uncle Bill dying. A piece of shrapnel that had been lodged near his heart had moved and killed him forty years later...the person who shot the gun as guilty in 1981 as he would have been had my uncle died in 1944.

I remember standing at the cemetery as the eerie sound of "Taps" drifted to my ears. I remember the Honor Guard who folded the flag, placed it in Aunt Audrey's outstretched hands, clicked his heels, and gave a sharp salute. Tears streamed down my face as I thought of the good natured, smiling man who had lived his life in excruciating pain so that the people of the world could live their lives in freedom.

I remember visiting the Vietnam Veteran's Memorial in Washington D.C., tears streaming down my face as I ran my fingers over the names of men that I'd never known. Yet they died, not only for their country, but so everyone could enjoy equal opportunity, freedom of speech, and liberty.

I remember standing at the North Wall in Windsor, Ontario, looking for anyone's name that I might know. I remember 1998 when vandals viciously hammered holes in this monument erected in the honor of Canada's Vietnam Veterans. Many veterans had fought long and hard for that monument.

I remember knowing a young man who would wake up in the night, screaming; reliving some horrific atrocity that he had witnessed in Vietnam.

I remember standing in another cemetery, tears streaming down my face as I watched my Uncle Bert's coffin being lowered into the ground, the sound of "Taps" drifting across the cemetery.

Another funeral—my father's. I remember the Ontario Provincial Police officer who stood at attention and saluted as the hearse carrying Dad's body to the cemetery passed by.

I remember 1996; I took my grandson to the cenotaph for Remembrance Day Services, vowing that he would always remember, just as I did.

I remember Remembrance Day 1999. I watched the ceremonies on TV. It was the first time in his life that my grandson and I had not attended the ceremonies together. He was in school—a tradition broken.

I remember, too, that when he came home from school, he was full of questions. Why had soldiers died for him? I tried to explain the best I could on his level. I also remember him asking me to pin my poppy on his shirt. He never wants anything pinned or stuck to his clothes. He gives the teacher a hard time when she tries to pin a nametag on him. It is just something he doesn't like. So you can imagine my surprise at his request. I will remember too, the way he walked around the house, chest pushed forward singing "O' Canada" for the soldiers who had died that he could be free. He sacrificed a fear to pay tribute to those men and women who paid the ultimate sacrifice. I cannot describe the pride I felt at that moment.

I remember brushing a tear from my eye when he told me he wanted to go to war and fight so the world could be free. I pray he never has to pay such a price. Now he is two years older and says he never wants there to be another war.

I will never forget September 11, 2001, when two planes flew into the north and south towers of the World Trade Center in New York City and a third into the Pentagon in Washington. A fourth plane crashed outside of Pittsburgh.

I will never forget the carnage of the streets of New York, the evacuations, and the men and women who were sent to New York and Washington to help with search and rescue efforts. I remember... Yes, I remember.

Author's Note: November 11 is Remembrance Day in Canada. I dedicate this article to veterans of all the Allied Nations and to the victims, survivors and those firemen, policemen, and other rescue workers who gave their lives when the terrorist attack occurred in the United States on September 11, 2001. May God bless us all.

Dear World Trade Center

By Traci Amor Draper
California, USA

Dear World Trade Center:

When I was 16 years old, I remember going to visit you. Remember how happy you were to see me? You were happy to see all the people who visited you that day. You were so proud of the view from the very top of your towers. I walked through the bottom floor with my friends and got lost while looking for the elevator that would take me to the very top. I couldn't wait to see the view that you provided. I had my camera around my neck, ready to snap the pictures that I would lovingly place in my photo album for my future grandchildren to look at.

I remember looking at the walls and the structure, so strong and indestructible. I had a doughnut at my favorite doughnut shop, Krispy Kreme Doughnuts. I sat at a table, looked around, and admired the beauty that surrounded me. I felt very safe within your arms.

My friends and I walked around and looked at all the shops within you, wishing we had more money to spend. Finally, we found the elevators that would take us to your top and fill us with the beauty that only you could provide. The elevator sped up to the top like a speeding bullet. It was the strangest feeling; our feet felt like they left the ground just a little bit, and we all felt a little taller inside that big, grand box.

We finally reached the top with a small thud and slowly exited onto the cement roof. We looked up at the clear blue sky and felt like we could touch the blueness right above us. We just stared up and smiled, feeling the warmth of the sun, which was a little warmer because we were so high up in the air.

I walked to the edge very slowly and looked around me. I could see Brooklyn, all of lower Manhattan, upper Manhattan, all the surrounding waters, the Statue of Liberty, and Ellis Island. I looked at the Empire State Building, noticing how small it seemed; that used to be the world's tallest building before you came along. You weren't the tallest anymore either, but there were two of you—so that made you the tallest in my eyes.

Today is September 11, 2001—I awoke this morning to see a plane in the side of one of your towers. I stood there in shock, unable to sit or even keep standing. As I stood there, you were hit with another airplane in your other tower, and I cried. I don't think I have stopped crying yet.

As I finally sat down to watch all of the events unfold, praying that they could repair you and all of your beauty, you started to fall. The first tower fell and I watched in horror as the second tower came shortly after. There would be no repair now.

I remembered being 16 years old, eating a doughnut at the World Trade Center—how safe I felt being within your arms. I could not even imagine how devastated you were to have fallen so easily and knowing that all of those people were inside of you thinking that they were safe in your strength. You must have started crying yourself when you realized how many lives had been taken with yours.

But it's okay World Trade Center—I promise those people were better off going with you than any other way. They will be remembered just as long as you will—forever.

There are two laser beams set up to go as high as you did. It is for all of us to remember that you stood there, in all of your glory, and will not be forgotten. It is also there to help those that were lost find their way home.

Please don't cry. We will cry for you and pray for you and all of those lost to us on this horrible day. But we will remain strong because even though you have fallen, you have left your strength for us to carry on. We thank you for that, World Trade Center. Perhaps we will never build a replica of you, but something that will always remind us of you in the many years to come.

My grandchildren will still see the photos I took that day so long ago; but they will know what happened to you, and they will go on because of your strength, too. Your strength and power will help generations to come. Every time I sit in the sun or tilt my head up to bask in the warmth, I will remember the warmth and safety you provided me that day when I was 16 years old.

The Lucky Ones

By April O'Herron
Ohio, USA

Everyone knows where they were when the Challenger blew up. No one will forget their surroundings when Kennedy was assassinated. I was in the dentist's chair, nearly upside down, on the morning of September 11, 2001. I still don't feel like I am right side up.

In the hours to come, the assaults on our senses came in unending torrents. There wasn't enough time to take in one slice of insanity before the next one came in. Names appeared on TV and computer screens. Did we know someone? Did we know someone who knows someone?

Schizophrenic feelings popped up at the oddest times. Why am I pumping gas while rescuers are searching for survivors? How can I be mulling over whether or not to mow my grass when military personnel are gearing up for moves across the country or the world? My 15-year-old daughter decided that she had to do something (too young to give blood and too broke to give money) and enlisted the two of us to assist with a local blood drive. Another relative emailed me blond jokes on the night of the 11th. "You have to keep your sense of humor," he said.

There are others who are walking this schizophrenic line, I've noticed. When I drove by a corner coffee shop the other day, their side glass window sported a somber note about an upcoming vigil and remembrance service with the date and time. I nearly swerved into a parked car when I saw their front glass window, however. It said, "Hunt 'em down and kill 'em all."

Never before have I seen the word "terror" so many times in one short span. The next time I see the word "rubble," I want it to refer to Barney, Fred Flintstone's pal.

And yes, I know life goes on. For some of us. The lucky ones.

We Fall

By Angie Ledbetter
Louisiana, USA

When the world crumbles around us,
Longing for peace calls.
Where terror reigns so ominous,
Panicked hearts do fall.
A dark day is forever made,
In the minds of all.
Hopes, dreams, and plans all gone today,
Like dried leaves in fall.
The end of innocence is now
For a nation tall.
It is time for all heads to bow.
To our knees we fall.

For all victims of terrorism

The Guilt Factor

By Shirley Kawa-Jump
Indiana, USA

It's the little things in my house that jolt my memory and bring me back to September 11. Before that day, these were mostly inconsequential objects that collected dust. The American flag that sits in a flowerpot by my desk, left over from the fourth of July. The picture of my husband from his days in the Navy, a vivid reminder of where he could be, had he stayed in the military. And, oddly enough, my treadmill. When the first plane crashed into the World Trade Center, I was on my treadmill, watching *Good Morning America*. When the second plane hit, I realized at the same time that this wasn't an accident and conversely that I was a thousand miles away from the tragedy, safe in the cornfield-dotted landscape of Indiana.

But when the reality of what happened finally hit me a second later, it was like a cement truck plowing through my heart. I stumbled off the treadmill and into a chair. I spent the entire day glued to the television. I hugged my son, worried about my daughter in school and my husband at work, and I watched. A couple of times, I went outside just to hear the quiet chirping of the birds and remind myself the world still existed.

There was no one I knew well on those planes, no one I'd ever shared coffee with in the towers. None of my friends were at the Pentagon; nobody I knew was involved. I had once done a phone interview with Father Grogan, the priest from

Easton, Massachusetts, who'd been on the second plane, but that had been more than 15 years ago and but a brief blip in his life and mine. My father's second office had been hit, but he was safe at home that day. That was as close as I'd come to being affected.

I watched the nation mourn and felt spurred into action. I made an appointment at the Red Cross, bought not one flag, but two, and installed the poles with pride. I held a candle on Friday night, comforted worried friends, cried with people who'd had a more direct loss than I had, and watched the news voraciously.

In the scheme of things, what I did was nothing. Even now, as the war plays out, I'm a spectator, not an actor. My job is to be aware, to pay attention to this life and history lesson in the making. I feel a surge of pride when Navy men and women stand on ship decks in their dress whites, off to fight a battle that has no end in sight. I listen to the anger and determination in the President's voice as he renews our spirits in the war on the horrible people who did this.

Lacing through all of this, though, is a feeling I'm not exactly proud of. I see the horror half a country away and am so grateful I live in Indiana, in the usually forgotten Midwest where the only value is in the land. I moved here five years ago from a suburb of Boston. On September 11, I'd never been more thankful I'd made that move.

The only signs of the war against terror are the National Guardsmen at our little airport and the barricades outside the Air Guard base. Otherwise, life here looks and smells the same. The farm reports still run on the radio. The neighbors still cut their lawns on Saturdays. The hunters still gear up for each season with new rifles and better camouflage.

In the coffee shops and around the water cooler, the conversation invariably drifts to the terror attacks, even now, months later. People probe gently at first, "Did you lose anyone?" And when the answer is no, they seem to sag with relief. They are not the only ones for whom this whole event seems surreal, distant.

I wonder if they feel as I do—guilty that there hasn't been a stronger toll in their lives. On an online list I belong to, there was a flurry of worried posts when Lisa Beamer was on television, talking about her heroic husband, Todd, who'd been part of the effort to overthrow the terrorists on the plane in Pittsburgh. Was it the same Lisa Beamer who was a member of our list, we wondered? Was there one of our own in this? But no, it turned out to be another Lisa, half a country from our Lisa.

The dollars I dropped into the Red Cross box, the flags I hung, the prayers I whispered, the tears I shed—none of it seems to be enough. And that bothers me, a constant needle in my side telling me I should be doing more. What more, I don't know. I feel guilty for going back to enjoying my life in the middle of nowhere. Guilty that I am so relieved my family was spared in the attacks. Guilty that my day-to-day focus is more on helping our business climb out of this economic decline than on the news reports. Guilty that all I can really do is wait for whatever comes next.

I have yet to get back on my treadmill. It's as if that represents my feelings of inadequacy, as if that would be the final step in returning to normal, and thus, what happened on September 11 would be forgotten. In the meantime, I keep flying my flag and saying prayers, watching the war on terror unfold from the safety of my living room, thousands of miles away. And hoping my small effort to help will make a difference to people whose pain I can barely imagine.

Better Than Superman

By Mae Hochstetler
Ohio, USA

When the first airliner hit Tower One of the World Trade Center on September 11, 2001, I was picking tomatoes in my Mom's garden. My baby played in the yard near me while the autumn sunshine warmed my back as I pulled ripe tomatoes from Mom's tomato plants. I carried the two pecks of tomatoes out to my minivan, then checked to see if Mom had anything else for me to do before I started home to begin the all-day process of canning tomato sauce.

"Come in here," Mom called, as she heard the cowbells hit the back door when the baby and I entered. In the parlor, she and my stepfather sat in shock. I looked at the television and saw smoke billowing out of the World Trade Center.

One of my favorite sites in New York City, the cherry on the top of the Big Apple skyline, as it always outshone the Empire State Building—the World Trade Center—was on fire. I remembered seeing it for the last time when I was pregnant with Baby Hope en route to the U.S. Open, remembered seeing the Twin Towers and the Manhattan skyline on our subway ride out of the city to Flushing.

My heart wrenched as I knew that I had to get back to my home and clean the tomatoes before the children's morning at preschool ended. I loaded the baby in the van and listened as the radio blared with the events of that morning.

As the reporter announced the crashing of the second tower by another airliner, the shocked old man driving the truck in front of me on Midlothian Blvd. stopped short. I hit the brake, and the two pecks of tomatoes flew across the floor of my van as the baby slept soundly in her car seat. Later that morning, with the baby asleep on the couch, I avoided the television, glad that the processing of tomatoes kept me busy. The whole event was too incredulous at that moment. I didn't want to deal with it or think about it while I was alone. I had to keep my wits about me for the sake of the children, who wouldn't understand the events that had transpired that morning.

While quartering the washed tomatoes into the big steel pots, I heard my husband's car in the driveway. Hugging me, he explained that the courthouse was closed because of the threat to government offices after the Pentagon was hit. With his arm about my hip, we watched the devastation on the television. We discussed how we didn't want our three preschoolers to see the constant replaying of the planes hitting the buildings, especially when their father was scheduled to fly to Vancouver in three days. It would be hard enough becoming a single parent of four children under five years for a week, but to add night terrors to it would only make matters worse. They would not be able to separate what happened at the World Trade Center or the Pentagon from the jet plane their father would travel on that week.

We determined the television would remain off until the children went to bed that night and we would turn on the radio and listen to the coverage there. I shut off the stove and let the tomatoes sit. Together we picked up our children from preschool, needing to see their little faces in a desperate way.

Later that afternoon, while the children played in the yard with their Daddy, I peeled garlic for pots of simmering tomatoes while the radio blared on about the destruction of the financial empire of the Western World that had inhabited the offices of the World Trade Center. I stirred the red sauce and thought of the fire trucks that responded that day that were now covered in ash as white as the shredded garlic peels that stuck to my fingers. Still, the shock was all too new. Allegations were made that it was Osama Bin Laden, and his terrorists but no one knew for certain where this act of hatred originated. I racked my brain considering who could do this. Why had they done it? Had they no shred of humanity?

I turned the crank on the sieve, mincing the cloves of garlic and cooked tomatoes so that the sauce would be separated into the pan below. As I watched the white clove of garlic mince into the sauce, I imagined the tons of mortar that fell that day, the crushing of bones and later of lives when the discovered deceased's families waited to be informed that their loved ones perished in this disaster.

When the children came back into the house, I forced back tears, trying not to cry in front of them taking turns at the sieve crank. I couldn't explain this to them today; I'd let them enjoy their day making spaghetti sauce and knowing dinner tomorrow would be pasta, one of their favorite meals. No, I couldn't explain it and at that point, none of us could. Prayer vigils were being formed and announced while schools were canceling activities. Life would stop for almost a week before anyone's lives returned to some sense of normalcy. After the events of September 11, 2001, our lives would never be the same again.

Threats of war from our President and retaliation from angry citizens upon their Arab-American neighbors emerged. I begged in my heart for life to return to how it was on Monday, wishing that Tuesday never occurred, that the world could start that day over again and someone would stop these mad men. *Where was Superman™ when we needed him?* I asked myself later while folding one of my four-year-old Matthew's super-hero T-shirts.

Since we returned to Youngstown a year ago, I had missed the city in a big way. I missed the hustle and bustle of daily life, the skyline, the arts, all of it—until that Tuesday. For once, I was glad to live in the small city of Youngstown, Ohio, where I was raised, near my family and canning tomatoes instead of going to work in Center-City Philadelphia.

I considered the rescue workers, whose lives had been lost trying to help others to safety. I thought of the No. 9 Firehouse down the street from me and how those firefighters brought their truck to Matthew's fourth birthday party. As a mother, I was grateful that they educated the children about fire safety and not to fear the firefighter in his full uniform but to come to him so he could take them to safety. I thought of how they always visit with my children on our summer walks to the library and what an integral part of the community our firehouse is in our borough of Brownlee Woods. If we had lost most of our firehouse as some precincts in New York had, it would have been a great loss to our neighborhood. Our firefighters and police officers are such an important part of our community. They keep us safe and teach our children how to be safe and to rely upon them in need.

Weeks later, the work of everyday life seems so mundane in the wake of this tragedy, as no work can compare to that of those at Ground Zero this last month, especially that of the New York Police and Fire Departments.

We still can't trust that the networks won't be continuously replaying the planes crashing into the World Trade Center, so we continue to censor the news programming from our children. My husband, Marcus, and I rise early in the morning to watch the news and go to bed late to get every morsel of information we can, relying on the radio throughout the day for information otherwise.

One morning, when I thought all the children were still asleep, I got another cup of coffee from the kitchen and returned to find my four-year-old Matthew standing in front of the television watching the replay of the towers' collapse.

"Mommy, what happened to that building?" he asked as the view was changed from the crumbling building to the workers at Ground Zero. I watched the firefighters on the television trying to formulate an explanation suitable for a four-year-old.

"Some really bad guys," I said, explaining to him with superhero talk, "crashed into those buildings and made them fall."

"Why?" he asked.

"Because they were mean."

"Were there people in the buildings?"

"Yes."

"Did a lot of Mommies and Daddies 'got died' in that building?"

"Yes, Matthew."

"Daddy used to work in a building like that when we lived in the city."

"Yes, he did."

"I'm glad he doesn't work there anymore."

I agreed with Matthew as he continued to watch the firefighters amid the news reports. Intrigued by Fisher Price's Rescue Heroes™, who are action figures of safety officers, policemen, firefighters, paramedics, and forest rangers, I knew who he was looking for on the broadcast.

"Is Wendy Waters™ and Billy Blazes™ there?" he asked regarding the firefighting pair who were his favorites of the Rescue Heroes™.

"Well, people like them. They're firefighters like the Rescue Heroes™." Matt watched the TV some more while I sipped my coffee.

"Mommy," he finally said at last, pointing to the firefighters on the television, "those Rescue Heroes™ are better than Superman™."

Matthew was right.

Even Superman™ couldn't stop this from happening. Nor could the rescue heroes of New York City, although they tried. They worked to save all that they could. Some perished among them, and some still work to find those comrades whom they've lost. And those who are called up into the Armed Forces will work until justice is met.

Since this event, I hold my children a little longer, like I'm sure most mothers do. I listen to their words with more interest, realizing they have contributions to make, even at four, three, and two years of age.

Every afternoon before we work on our ABC's & 123's, Matthew insists that we flip through the news channels to see if the workers at Ground Zero, whom he refers to as the "Real Rescue Heroes," are being televised. One day, a bit exasperated from his lingering in front of the television, I said to Matthew, "They're not Wendy Waters™ and Billy Blazes™, you know."

"I know," he replied, turning off the television, "they're tougher, because they're the Real Rescue Heroes."

As I thought about this, I realized his wisdom. Anyone who would return day after day to continue his or her efforts was tough.

"Tougher than Batman™?"

Matthew rolled his green eyes at me and replied, "Mom, the Real Rescue Heroes™ are tougher than Batman™ and Superman™ put together. Well, and maybe the Power Rangers™, too."

I'm Scared, I'm Sad, I'm Proud, I'm Free: A Child's Perspective on 9/11

By Rebecca Spence
New Jersey, USA

The crashes were big.
The tall, tall buildings fell down.
My Mom and Dad were crying.
I felt afraid.
The grown-ups said bad people crashed the planes.
I'm scared the bad people will come and hurt me.
My Mom and Dad say that won't happen.
They say they will protect me.
They say we have lots of brave policemen and policewomen
to protect us.
And then they hug me.
And kiss me.
And tell me they love me.
They do that all the time now.
And then I feel a little bit better.

The grown-ups say a lot of people died in the crashes.
They even knew some of the people who died.
That makes me feel very, very sad.
My Mom and Dad say it's okay to feel sad.
Even to cry.
They say crying can make you feel a little bit better some-
times.

And then they hug me.
And kiss me.
And tell me they love me.
They do that all the time now.
And then I feel a little bit better.

The grown-ups say many brave firefighters and police and
emergency workers
and even just regular people saved thousands of lives.
Many of them gave their lives to save others.
My Mom and Dad say they are heroes.
I feel proud of our heroes.
My Mom and Dad say it's good to feel proud of our heroes.
They say these heroes should never be forgotten.
And then they hug me.
And kiss me.
And tell me they love me.
They do that all the time now.
And then I feel a little bit better.

The grown-ups say this was an attack on our country.
They say it was an attack on freedom and goodness.
They say we are at war.
I feel confused about that because I don't really understand
what this war is all about.
My Mom and Dad say I'll understand more someday.
They say all I need to know right now is that I am very lucky
to live in such a great country.
They say freedom is worth fighting for.
And then they hug me.
And kiss me.
And tell me they love me.
They do that all the time now.
And then I feel a little bit better.

Note: This was not written by a child. This is one mother's reflection, based on observations and conversations with her children and others, of what some young children were experiencing and feeling in response to the events of 9/11.

9-11-01

By Kari Abate
Illinois, USA

In the kitchen, my hands
Skim neat stacks of plates
Stowed safely in the cupboard.
I count their sturdy bones,
Marvel how light reflects
Off the rims, one chipped.
Outside, a lawnmower drones
Its familiar, sleepy sound,
Restores order to a front yard.
The sky is siren blue.
The sun moils on.
Rich, protected,
We munch on chocolate cupcakes
In our pajamas.
Emily says
Wow, look at the fire, Mama—
And I realize I've been careless with the television,
Brought its arsenal into our living room
Where I sift through the debris of shock,
Sort the bodies with inertia,
Measure each breath in silence.

Terror in the Flames

By Jennifer LB Leese
Maryland, USA

Twisted minds prepared for their death.
    And in the blink of an eye,
    they left the world behind.
But what about the ones that didn't plan to die?
The world has forever changed.
Many lives were taken by force
and for the ones that have perished,
    what is our recourse?
Heartbreak, fear, and destruction,
    what is it that they yearned?
They caused chaos in so many hearts.
Debris rained, as the towers burned.
We saw terror in the flames.
Gray now blankets our Nation.
So many lost; so many hurt.
    What were their names?

The River Keeps Flowing

By Mary Lane Cryns
California, USA

Yesterday my daughter Megan begged me to take her swimming at the Tule River. Brian, Matt, and Brettany, friends from the neighborhood, wanted to go, too. At first I thought about going to church and praying for all of the people who left this earth last week, even though I hadn't been to church in ages.

But I decided the kids could use some fun time, too, and opted to take them to the river instead. When we got there, even the kids noticed that the river water, which was usually warmed by the afternoon sun, was a lot colder than usual. It took us a while to get used to the water, but in no time we were all splashing, swimming, and having a good time.

I climbed up onto a rock in the warm afternoon sun and looked over at the trickling water and the trees and listened to the water flowing into the open part of the river where we had been swimming and watched it move down, forever flowing.

It was a peaceful moment, and I thought about how this river keeps flowing, no matter what. The fish still swim in the river and the birds and butterflies fly. And the kids play, swim, and have fun. I can't stop that from happening; none of us can. Precious lives are lost, yet we still live, we prevail.

4

The Spirit of America: Hope for the Future

"As we join to end the scourge of terrorism, let us also unite to seize the opportunities we share to build a world of peace, prosperity, and democracy."

— *Colin L. Powell*
Secretary of State

What I've Learned

By Victoria Walker
Florida, USA

On the morning of September 11, 2001, the citizens of America saw the sun rise just as it had each day before. They planned to go about their normal routines, never imagining that things would never again be the same. After the devastating attacks on America that awful Tuesday morning, we awoke to a different world on September 12—a world where people are a little more fearful about their tomorrows, a little sadder for the suffering of others, and a lot more willing to try to make a difference.

Despite our losses, our heartaches, and our fears, some positive outcomes have resulted from these events—outcomes that the terrorist who wished to destroy us could never have anticipated, nor comprehended. There is renewed patriotism in America. Our stars & stripes are flying proudly from churches, businesses, homes, cars, and schools. Neighbors are taking an extra moment to wave at each other; hurried citizens are slowing down, spending a little more time with their family and friends and being a little more kind. In times of sorrow, we realize what is truly important.

This is what I've learned in the sorrowful days that followed September 11, 2001:

I've learned that life is too short to stay in an unhappy marriage, a job you hate, a town you hate, or any situation that makes you unhappy. If it doesn't make you happy now, you need to move forward and find something that does make you happy. You may never get another chance. Live your life today! Be happy today!

I've learned to value my family and friends far more today than I did before the September 11 attacks. Sometimes, we get so busy in life that we "don't have time" to spend with our family and friends. But there is nothing more important. Turn off the TV, the computer, put down your book, and talk to your loved ones. They may not be here tomorrow!

I've learned what a hero really is. Merriam-Webster Dictionary says that a hero is "one that shows great courage." Someone that is willing to crash an airplane into a field—knowing that he is going to die, just so he may save the lives of others—strangers that he has never met—*that is a hero*. Someone willing to run into a burning skyscraper to help frightened strangers find their way to safety, even if it means risking his own life—*that, too, is a hero*. A President with a tear in his eye gently comforting his nation while promising justice to those who hurt his country—*he, too, is a hero.*

I've learned that people really do care about each other—they really do care what is happening in the world. People can put aside their differences and work together for the good of mankind.

I've learned that true leaders and true heroes emerge in times of crisis.

I've learned that you realize who your true friends are in times of adversity. A friend whom I've known since childhood emailed me a few days after September 11 to say how much she has valued our friendship over the past 20 years—and that she wanted to tell me now just in case she never got another chance. That's a true friend!

I've learned that we all, worldwide, must overlook our differences and work together—if we ever truly expect to live in a peaceful world.

I've learned to renew my relationship with God, not to put it off until tomorrow—tomorrow may be too late!

Finally, I've learned that sometimes we all need to reach out and help our neighbor, even if they haven't asked for help. Imagine what a better world this would be if everyone performed one random act of kindness every day!

The Soul of America

By Stefani Barbero
North Carolina, USA

When I was a child, my parents took me to every monument and historical site within a day's drive of our western Maryland home. They felt it was important to know our nation's history, to understand the foundations of our society, to appreciate what we as a nation believe.

We visited the Lincoln Memorial, toured the Capitol, and trekked endlessly through the exhibits of the Smithsonian. And despite my tired nine-year-old legs, I began to understand the deeper meanings behind these buildings.

Even as an adult, as I stand atop the steps of the Lincoln Memorial, I feel a lump in my throat as I read the words above President Lincoln's likeness—healing words from a difficult time, perhaps the most divisive time in our collective history. They came from deep within the heart of a great and compassionate man, a man who hated war but knew that it must be fought to save the soul of our nation. These words speak of sacrifice, but also of hope and faith and a profound belief in the guiding principles upon which our country was founded.

Those weekend trips with my family instilled in me a deep love for our nation's history, but also an intense appreciation for human achievement. For me, the graceful curve of the Capitol dome, the preserved homes of our great presidents, and the memorials we've constructed on the Washington mall are monuments to freedom, justice, equality, and every human virtue. We have chosen the best of humanity to celebrate and revere, and it is a constant source of pride for me. We are a nation built on principle, unlike any other.

As I travel throughout our country, I find monuments to human achievement in every city, but nowhere are these accomplishments more prominently displayed than in New York. The very skyline of that great city is all the evidence I need that all things are possible.

When I went to New York for the first time a few years ago, I made it a point to visit the Empire State Building. As I marveled at the polished marble in the lobby, I thought only of the architect who imagined such a beautiful building, the businessmen who had the courage and vision to finance such an outlandish project, and the countless workmen who risked their lives to do what had never been done before.

By comparison, the twin towers of the World Trade Center were not beautiful, but they, too, filled me with awe. I stood on the sidewalk craning my neck to see the top, and for the first time in my life the phrase "dizzying heights" made perfect sense. From the rooftop, all of Manhattan was laid out before me, and I was once again stunned by the enormity of human achievement that is New York.

The sheer size of the World Trade Center seemed to suggest that even the laws of physics can be defied if only we have vision, ingenuity, and perseverance. They were not beautiful buildings, but they were monuments to humanity, nonetheless.

On the morning of September 11, it took less than an hour to destroy those monuments. Like most Americans, I watched the television in horror as one tower collapsed, and then the other. They seemed to fold in on themselves like the calculated implosion of a condemned building.

But these buildings were not destroyed in the name of progress. They were destroyed in the name of hatred and injustice and all that is evil. In many ways, the World Trade Center had represented to me the best of humanity, and their destruction offered me a glimpse of the worst.

The day after this tragedy a disturbing reality began sinking in—as boundless as our capacity for achievement is, our capacity for evil is just as great.

Though I have watched the news coverage for hours on end, I have not grown accustomed to the gaping hole at the lower tip of Manhattan. I see the skyline on my television screen, and I think, *That's not the Manhattan I know.*

This isn't the America I know.

Just a short time ago the notion that a single terrorist attack within our borders could take the lives of thousands of Americans was so far-fetched that it seemed only Hollywood could pull it off. But that Tuesday morning those thousands of people did just what I did. They got up, got dressed, had their coffee, and went to work. And they became victims—targets of a terrorist attack. They had committed no crime, no sin. They were simply Americans, and that was reason enough.

This is the America my children will know.

With the smoke not yet cleared in New York, it's easy for me to believe that my expectations of safety and justice, too, have collapsed, and that, like the World Trade Center, they have become nothing but a gaping, smoldering hole.

And yet, I still believe in America and all the principles on which it was founded. I believe in humanity and all that we have achieved. And I believe that freedom, justice, and compassion are more powerful than any terrorist's weapon.

The illusion of complete safety and isolation from the world's violence may be gone, but my appreciation for human achievement in all its many forms remains. Some day I hope to pass it on to my children, just as my parents passed it on to me.

Even through my fear and uncertainty, I know that I will take my children to the observation deck of the Empire State Building to marvel at the power of hard work. I will take them to the Lincoln Memorial to remind them that one man can change the world. And I will take them to where the World Trade Center used to stand to prove to them that the soul of this nation is stronger than all the evil in the world.

In my heart I know that this government "of the people, by the people, for the people" shall not perish.

Good Versus Evil

By Joyce Jace
New Mexico, USA

❝Honey? Sit here and watch this with me," I instructed my nine-year-old son. We had been on our way out the door to school. He dutifully sat on the floor, and we watched over and over again the footage of the planes slamming into the towers.

"Is that the Empire State Building next to it?" he asked innocently. I hushed him and told him just to listen. The images just were not sinking in. I remember just shaking my head from side to side.

We got into the van to leave. I asked him what he thought about what he had just seen. In his typical "Mom, I can tell you're upset so I'll just crack a joke," style he said something silly. I reprimanded him and told him this was not a joking matter.

"Sorry, Mom. I saw two planes crash into two buildings."

"Do you understand how many people will die from those crashes?"

"Yes mom. Will something like that happen to me?"

"No, son. You are safe. Those were the acts of terrorists."

"What are terrorists?"

"Do you remember what I've always told you? There are some people in this world that hurt others. And do you remember that I've always told you that we cannot control how other people behave?"

"Yes, Mom. And you've also told me that there are more good people than bad people in this world and my job is to find those good people to share my life."

"That's right, honey. We cannot control those that are evil. We can only control our own behavior."

There was a long, pregnant pause between us as I continued to drive.

I looked over at him playing his handheld video game and stroked his hair.

"I love you, son. We're going to be okay."

"Mom? Why do those terrorists do that?"

"There are just some people in this world who hold their religious beliefs above the value of a human life. Their religion gives them permission to kill others."

"Does our religion do that, Mom? Would we do that for Buddha?"

"What is the greatest thing that Buddha has taught us? To do no harm. No son, Buddha would never allow us to harm any living creature."

"I like Buddha, Mom."

"I know. Me, too."

He reached over to his door, picked up his miniature statue of Buddha, and looked at it.

"Mom? What do you suppose is in the knapsack he carries?"

"I'm not sure. What do you think?"

"Well, maybe some food and water and one more robe. You told me all his possessions are carried in that sack and that he didn't own anything else."

"That's right, honey. Things don't matter. Only people. And we don't care what those people look like. We judge those people for what's in their…what?" I asked, waiting for him to fill in the blank.

"Uh. In their brain?" he remarked, with that mischievous smile that tells me I've asked him a dumb question.

"Just kiddin' mom. We judge people by what's in their heart."

I gave him an extra kiss that morning. I had done a good job of teaching him from an early age that there is indeed good and evil in this world. And that there always will be. He understands that that evil may or may not touch him and me. He also understands that we cannot control what happens to us, day in and day out.

We can control how we treat others and we can control our steadfast belief in the sanctity of life down to the tiniest creature. Anything beyond that is out of our control. We don't worry about it, nor do we fear it. We live each day, each moment, as if it's our last because we cannot ever know what's up ahead. And that's okay.

Yesterday They Fell

By April Lee Schmidt
Alabama, USA

Yesterday they fell—
    Symbols of America's
Greatness, power and strength,
    Lay in rubble all around.
Buildings only expressed faith—
    It is in God America trusts.
Her strength is in our hearts, our minds;
    Her power in our hands.
America dropped to her knees
    In prayer, not humility.
The symbols are not her strength
    It is in God America Trusts.
The shadow of death fell—
    Be not afraid for God is with her.
The rod and staff do comfort us;
    Goodness and mercy abound.
We are never alone—because
    It is in God America Trusts.

In a New York Minute

By Mary Dixon Lebeau
New Jersey, USA

The wind shifted, the skyline collapsed, and our priorities changed.

You needn't look far to see evidence of that. All you have to do is walk down the streets of your hometown and take note of the flags and banners, the star-spangled wishes and prayers of a country united in grief, united in hope. A country whose people seemed oblivious to each other mere days ago, but are now holding each other up or hanging on to each other's hand.

On Sunday, I went to church. Now, I must admit to being a rather sporadic churchgoer. There were years when I was a holiday Catholic, showing my face on Christmas and Easter and not dropping by too often during those weeks in between. I guess I went through a period when "church" seemed like a good idea in theory, but I found difficulty making a commitment in practice. In the past few months—at the request of one of my sons—my attendance record has improved. My children and I attend mass on Sunday pretty regularly now, but in all honesty, I never felt part of the community. It was like I was an interloper, allowed to watch the festivities but never really a part of it all.

Until last week.

My church—like most around the country—was full last week, as people turned back to God for answers and comfort, healing and hope. But despite the numbers who tried to squeeze into the pews, there seemed to be no animosity, no resentment from the "regulars" and the "foxhole Christians." Instead, people embraced each other, found strength in those numbers, and held hands during the "Our Father." Before we left the building, the choir led the congregation through every verse of "America, the Beautiful" as someone up front unfurled an American flag. I lost it right there, broke down and wept, and didn't feel self-conscious at all.

After all, everyone there understood. Everyone there was family.

There's a Don Henley song that says, "In a New York minute, everything can change." I guess we all know that by now. Our President told us to resume business as usual, and we try our best to do that, but I'm not sure what "usual" is any more. One thing I do know is that it will never be like before.

And I think this is a good thing. I enjoyed the casual freedom we once took for granted, but now we seem to have a deeper appreciation, a deeper understanding of how special and wonderful our country was—and is. We won't let the smoke blind us to the beauty that still remains—and the beauty that is springing up from the ashes. We won't let fear steal away our birthright.

For me, it also means a change in the very words I use. I remember, just a month ago, a co-worker telling us how he was stuck in traffic for an hour or so while making his trek home to Vineland from our Thorofare office. "Bumper to bumper, going nowhere," he told us. "It was horrible."

But that was before we learned what "horrible" really was. Back then, we groused about long lines, grumbled about the neighbor's kids running across the lawn, complained about our lack of choices at the vending machine. And of course, I know we'll get back to all that as we make our way through the debris to "business as usual." Still, I think we'll be more conscious of how meaningless these things really are.

We've learned the true definition of "horrible," all in a New York minute.

But in that same minute, we learned a new meaning of the word "hero." All my old heroes have diminished somehow as we see proof of true heroism all around us. How can we tout a singer or an athlete as a hero now, when men and women have risked their own lives in order to help or save others? There's a difference between "good guys" and "heroes"—and that difference was personified in the firefighters, policemen, and "just plain folks" who felt compelled to be there at ground zero, doing what they could to pick up the pieces.

"The amazing thing is, our husbands were ordinary men who dipped into their character or their faith to do something extraordinary," said Lisa Beamer during a *Good Morning America* interview this week.

She and Lyzbeth Glick were speaking about their husbands. Todd Beamer and Jeremy Glick are two of the passengers believed to have fought the hijackers of Flight 93, forcing the crash into a Pennsylvania field and possibly saving others who would have been victims if the flight had reached the hijackers' target.

Yes, it is amazing. It's the stuff of heroes, and all of these heroes deserve the respect, the gratitude, and the love of a nation. It's the stuff that makes us want to do something, even now, to help our fellow countrymen, to take those baby steps into the future.

It's the stuff that makes up this country. And as the rubble clears and those hard decisions are made, let's continue to help each other dip into that stuff.

9-11: An Irish Perspective

By Nancy Baker
Texas, USA

Ireland: The land of shamrocks, leprechauns, and people of hospitality, generosity, and compassion. We learned about the people of Ireland on September 11, 2001, and the days following. This was our dream vacation, the one we had planned for years. We arrived at Shannon on September 10 and spent the day recovering from jet lag. September 11 was spent traversing the land of a hundred shades of green and desperately trying to become skilled at driving on the left-hand side of the road.

We were registering at the Lake Hotel in Killarney, our American accents prominent, when the desk clerk solicitously asked, "Have you heard about the World Trade Center?" We suffered all the shock and dismay Americans at home experienced. We were glued to the television. Over and over we witnessed the horrific impact of the airplanes and the disaster left in their wake. We felt isolated, lost, orphaned. Our homeland was being attacked, and we were in a foreign country. We were unable to get in touch with our family. Questions filled our minds: *When would we be able to get home? Should we continue with our trip? Whom do we ask?*

Even on this very first day, we became the objects of Irish caring. The hotel staff wrote down the e-mail addresses of our family and began trying to contact them for us. Irish guests at the hotel approached us and expressed their sorrow for our loss and their support of our country. As we ate dinner that evening, we lamented our inability to get home. What would we do when our reservations ran out? Where will we go? "Our home," came the answer from the table next to ours. "You're welcome to stay with us until you can make arrangements." We were just beginning to experience Irish hospitality. Smiling Irish eyes assured us of their sincerity.

The next morning we could think of nothing else, and prayer seemed to be the best avenue to pursue. We drove to the Franciscan Cathedral in downtown Killarney. The solace and peace of the ancient church soothed us. I noticed people lighting candles and then, a hand-lettered sign above the rack holding the votive candles: "For the Americans." Tears came unbidden.

Walking back to our car, I was suddenly, embarrassingly, struck with the need for a rest room. There were no businesses in sight except for a funeral home. Unlikely as it seemed, I simply had to find a rest room.

"Of course, of course, come in."

When I returned to the reception area after my emergency stop, my husband was sipping a cup of tea and the funeral director was offering his condolences, our American accents having once again given us away.

"You know all of us Irish are half American. I have family in Boston." His Irish eyes held genuine compassion.

"And, all of us Americans are half Irish. I just wish I had family in Ireland," I replied.

"You do. Ask any of us."

Since, for the present time, we were unable to return home, we continued on our itinerary but kept closely in touch with the American Embassy, Aer Lingus, and our family at home, whom we had finally been able to reach. Everywhere we went there were books of condolences signed by the Irish and tourists alike.

On the National Day of Prayer we stopped at a church at the appointed time. I was astonished to see wreaths and funeral sprays entirely covering the steps. At first I thought there was a funeral in process. In a sense there was, although there was no body. "These flowers are for our American friends. May they rest in peace. God bless America," one note read.

On the National Day of Mourning we could not find a single store open in Kinsale. In fact, we could not even find a place to eat. So we fasted for the dead, and our Irish family refrained from work in honor of fallen Americans.

We love lighthouses and wanted to visit the one at Old Head. However, it is part of a very exclusive golf course, and one must be a member to enter. We thought we might get a glimpse of it and drove to the coast.

The views were spectacular. Though Ireland is a small country, there is a feeling of vastness about it. We were touched once again to see flags flying at half mast at the entrance to the golf course. The lighthouse could be seen in the distance, and we stopped to take a picture. The guard at the gate approached and informed us that only members were allowed past this point.

"Just wanted to get a photograph of the lighthouse and the flags," my husband responded.

The guard looked up with surprise, "Oh, you're American."

"How did you guess?" my husband chuckled, using his best Texas drawl.

The laughing Irish eyes again. "Well then, perhaps you would like to purchase something at the pro-shop?" He winked. Clearly, that was the place to get the best view of the lighthouse. On the way out, we thanked him for bending the rules a little for us. "I just wanted to do something, anything for America, Americans."

Perhaps the place where we felt the most prayerful was at the Cliffs of Mohr. These 300,000 million-year-old cliffs inspire reverence. In spite of the thousands of tourists that visit them daily, there is a holiness at this place that reminds one of being in church, only this is an awesome outdoor cathedral. At the beginning of the walkway stood an American flag with a book of condolence beside it and a line of people waiting to sign the book.

When we arrived home some three weeks later, our daughter met us at the airport with tears and a bouquet of long stemmed American Beauty roses.

"Welcome home, Mom and Dad."

I felt tears start in the back of my eyes, too. "Thank you, sweetheart. It's so good to be home. God bless America."

"And God bless our Irish family, too," my husband added, for we had come to think of the smiling Irish as kinsmen.

Mother America

By Flor Cardona
Arizona, USA

How did the sister feel
when the brother was torn from her?
How did the mother live
with the sacrifice of seeing
how the badness of one person
took her babies
and tore them from her womb?
Her twins are gone.
She sacrificed her life
and her other children
to rebuild hope,
because without them
she is hopeless,
empty,
like one part of her heart
which has been torn
will always be.
She can't see clearly—
the dark cloud is still in her way.
It is made of dust and selfishness.
of people
who don't believe in the freedom
that we are blessed with
from our Mother America.

911: A Cry for Tolerance

By Barbara Jane Russell Robinson
Florida, USA

History is alive, well, and thriving. It is what makes life important. Without history, there would be no memories, nothing important in and to life. History is the heart and soul of America—it lives on in each of us. History is part of the past in that we learn from our mistakes and use what we've learned to improve our future. History is the present in that we are making history as we live our lives each day. History is the future in that what we do today shapes who and what we become tomorrow. As such, the September 11 tragedy should not be pushed into the backs of our minds and forgotten. To choose to forget would mean forgetting the many victims. Choosing to remember, as a lesson in time and history, means that the victims who lost their lives on that tragic day did not die in vain.

Past history has affected my life through my experiences—through the mistakes I have made and learned from, through obstacles I have had to overcome, through successes I have experienced, through school experiences and through past teachers. History is the greatest teacher of all. For one can learn how to use the knowledge gained through life's experiences to improve the future.

Past experiences have made me the person I am today. Past teachers have taught me more than textbooks and have influenced me to become the teacher I am today. There is an expression, "History repeats itself." I believe this is true and a reality in life; we cannot forget September 11.

Present history in the making affects me on a daily basis. As the events of September 11 unfolded, I found myself in a state of shock. I had just finished teaching my first-hour class and was planning second hour. It was then, as I ran an errand to the front office of Denn John Middle School in Kissimmee, Florida, that I learned about the horrible early morning events that were in progress. My heart sank as I silently prayed for the victims, their families, and our nation.

Ironically my errand to the office involved sharing a letter from a parent with my assistant principal. The letter told me to ask God for help, and I had replied that I always did, and He always answered my prayers. I was sharing my response with my assistant principal before sending it to the parent. It was in the midst of this that I saw pictures on television of the airplanes crashing into the beloved Twin Towers in New York City. Immediately, I thought about the President who was speaking at another school in Florida, and I asked the good Lord to give us all the protection of His rear guard.

The future of our country was at stake. Students of today will be tomorrow's future, our country's future. Therefore, they are our history and our future. History is alive, well, and thriving. It is the heartbeat of America. History will always linger in our hearts and minds, with our memories and experiences, making us the unique human beings we are. We are all individuals made up of our own unique blend of personal history that affects the past, the present, and the future of our lives and our country. It is our differences that make us unique and special, and it is time people start appreciating one another for those unique differences that make the melting pot of America. Like a specially handcrafted patchwork quilt made by our grandmothers and like Dolly Parton's coat of many colors, it is that very uniqueness and diversity that makes America one great nation under God. We, as Americans, should be proud and stand united together to keep our nation strong and undivided, therefore, keeping it unconquered. In my heart, I see September 11 as a cry for the world to wake up—a wake-up call for tolerance, understanding, and acceptance of people for who they are and for being part of our great nation, America—an America we can be proud to call our home. For we were all created equally in God's eyes, in His own image. Should that not be good enough for us mere humans to accept?

History was in the making September 11, 2001, as we watched in horror the tragedy unfolding before our eyes on the news. The tragedy of September 11 certainly affected all of us in our dearly beloved country; but our star-spangled banner yet waves, and we are still the home of the brave!

Sifting Through the Ashes

By Kymberli W. Brady
California, USA

As the dust continues to settle in America and a true glimpse of the terror that ensued on September 11 starts to reveal the devastation of our homeland that violated our way of life, I take pride in people all over the country as we band together in the process of rebuilding. Once strangers, now friends and co-patriots, we are more united as a family and a nation.

By their act of cowardice, terrorists have succeeded only in bringing us closer together. The compassion of Americans everywhere has and continues to be shadowed only by the determination to make this great land of ours better than before. I realize I am part of the birth of a new nation and am filled with a new dream and a grander purpose.

While some are in the throes of rebuilding their homes and their lives, others, including me, begin rebuilding our country's heartstrings. I am reminded every day of the reason why I love this great land. I think of my busy schedule that up to now took priority over the world outside my own personal agenda, and I stop to watch children as they painstakingly poke red, white, and blue plastic cups into chain link fences until a perfect image of our nations' flag glistens under the autumn sun. I drive through one neighborhood after another, losing myself in patriotic displays of flags, ribbons, and signs reminiscent of a summer 4th of July celebration, only with much more pride than I can remember having ever seen before. For the first time in history, the colors of our country are now the colors of choice among many nations as the world bands together in displays of unity for a common cause—peace.

My journeys into each day bring welcome additions that serve as reminders of a country in mourning and the healing that is underway. People stand on street corners waving American flags, while the busy world stops thinking about rushing to their next meeting long enough to honk in genuine support. High school kids successfully usher perfectly clean cars into make-shift car washes in an effort to help raise money for the victims. I must admit I've more than willingly allowed them to convince me that my car needed another once over as I realized my pride in the fact that they are taking a proactive approach to healing in a world where they have no control. This is true American resolve at its best.

I am blessed to have been privy to many gatherings and rallies in memory of the fallen. New heroes, waiting in the wings, are now taking center stage in this ongoing saga. I reflect upon one such event, a unity rally at a local middle school, where 2,000 children proudly hung the flags from over 75 countries around the perimeter of their school. They wanted desperately to do something to help, as they were too young to give blood, and decided to turn their campus into a teddy bear factory. The determination of these children, as they raised $14,000 on their own so they could make teddy bears for the children of New York, has been nothing short of awe-inspiring. I am comforted in the knowledge that they will be our future leaders and make us proud parents, as well as Americans.

"These terrorists can shake the foundations of our largest buildings, but they cannot shake our resolve." As the words of President George W. Bush reverberate within me, I think about the resolve we, as a nation, have given birth to since that fateful day and how it will hold us together during the months and years ahead.

As a mother, I turn now to the task at hand in the war for freedom and ponder the letter my high school friend, Robyn, shared with me from her son—his last letter to her as he deployed to Afghanistan to defend our freedom. It suddenly occurred to me that, had I started my family when she did, I might very well have received a similar letter from my son. I take comfort in the fact that my son is only seven years old and to a great deal sheltered from all of this, but I feel her pain. I feel her fear as if it were my own. I can only imagine, as a mother, how it must feel to let your child go while facing the reality that you may never see him again. Her only solace is that letter in which he, for the first time, thanked her for all the sacrifices she made for him and told her that he had never really known before now how much he loved her and she him. He apologized for the fact that it took him 21 years to realize the kind of bond they shared, and told her how he would use that bond as his strength. His last words to her were these:

> *"Well, it's time for me to go and try and make the world a better place.*
>
> *"I love you, Mom, and will have you and the Lord Jesus in my heart while I am there."*

I wonder if—had I been put in the position of sending my son off to war—I would have the strength and acceptance she has displayed. She and every other mother in this situation have become my new heroes, role models I never thought about before. Robyn holds on tightly to that letter now, one of many such letters received from mothers all over the country, her heart heavy with the weight of a nation and clinging to each word in each precious letter and the hope that their children will return home safely. I pray that they do.

My greatest strength is that I truly love my life in this country. I have visited many others and experienced their cultures. But there is something about American soil that welcomes me home with open arms. I can breathe freely again once home, because I know her stars and stripes will protect me like a warm blanket on a wintry night. Life is full of unexpected, unimaginable moments. But it is also full of unexpected, wonderful memories. I take comfort in knowing that whatever this world has to offer, I will savor each breath. Whatever goals I achieve and obstacles I encounter, whoever I meet along the way, and what I will and won't get to do in this lifetime, I know each will be met with a newfound passion for living this life God had so graciously given me, taking small bites, and savoring each one. I am truly blessed and proud to be an American.

My belief is that we must band together and pick up the pieces as a nation so that we may continue to stand tall and proud. Each one of us lost something that sad day and share in the grief it has caused. We now face the task of setting an example for others, for the eyes of the world will be watching as we struggle to come to terms with this travesty. We now realize how fragile we are as a free society in a world riddled with terrorists. Hopefully, we will learn a valuable lesson from this as we, not as a country, but as a world, need to unite in an effort to ensure future peace for our children and the continued existence of the human race. We will survive and thrive.

My deepest sympathies go out to the families who lost loved ones on that dark day. I will think of them when welcoming each new day, as it will be theirs, too. Every moment I now take to stop and think of the true importance of my life, I will be reminded of those who lost theirs, as they have awakened a higher purpose in my soul.

I dedicate these words to every life lost in this tragedy. From the firemen, police officers, and volunteers who put their lives on the line to aid their countrymen and didn't make it in the end, to the fathers, mothers, brothers, sisters, sons, daughters, and friends overseas defending our freedom today. I will forever remember you all for your courage.

Darkness

By Gwen Morrison
Ontario, Canada

In the aftermath of darkness,
 I see a glimmer of hope
Shining down from above.
It soothes me;
It comforts me.
I breathe in its glory,
Drawing it deep within me,
Storing it along with the sadness
To overcome,
To understand.
I will never forget
The horrors of that day.
It resonates on the faces
Of strangers that pass by.
It's there
In their hearts
Where it will remain forever—
A reminder that we can break,
But we can endure
With love,
With unity.
Hearts are breaking
Around the world
For all that have suffered

And the pain yet to come.
But we must survive.
We must live on.
Our future depends on it.
Don't let terror win—
For love is stronger.
Love lives on
Forever.

God Grant Me the Serenity...

By Jim Donovan
Pennsylvania, USA

We all have our ways of dealing with the terrible tragedy that befell America on September 11, 2001. As an author and motivational speaker, I felt compelled to say something to try to help others through this time. During the days of processing my own grief, I found myself going back to an old and trusted friend, the Serenity Prayer. While the authorship of this simple, yet powerful prayer is unknown, it is copyrighted in the name of theologian Reinhold Niebuhr (1892-1971), who gave it to Bill Wilson, co-founder of Alcoholics Anonymous, and it is used to this day to help people in recovery. I found it a great comfort to me personally during this difficult time. Here is the prayer and some thoughts as to how we might use its wisdom to help us in our national healing.

God Grant Me ...

The Serenity...

To Accept the things I cannot change

America was attacked by terrorists and it is devastating. Too many people have been killed or injured, properties have been destroyed, and businesses damaged—perhaps beyond repair. Families have been torn apart, children left without a father or mother, husbands and wives missing a spouse, and parents missing children. This is a terrible tragedy, the likes of which we have never seen in the United States before.

The Courage to change the things I can

We cannot change what happened. But we can change is how we react to this. We can join the masses calling for retaliation and strike out at whatever enemy, real or imagined, is nearby, much like a mad dog would, or we can be courageous enough to stand tall as beacons of light holding, in our hearts, thoughts of peace and healing.

Do not think for a moment that I am taking any of this lightly. I am as outraged as you, however, I feel we can serve the cause for good more effectively by helping to heal both ourselves, our loved ones, and the world we live in. We have all been affected by this tragedy. There is no doubt about that.

As a native New Yorker, I am especially hurt and outraged at what has taken place. I have slept, feeling safe and secure, in the Marriott Hotel that is no more. I have browsed and shopped, joyously, in the Border's bookstore that is now part of the rubble. My wife once worked in the Telephone Company building, at 140 West Street, across the street from the WTC. This pain will take time to heal. Only time can heal a pain this severe.

In the meantime, we can only do what we can do. Now is a time that we can shift our thoughts away from the disaster and toward the good in our lives. We can be thankful for whatever we have and perhaps be a little more appreciative of our loved ones. Perhaps we could be a little more tolerant of the little bumps in our lives, realizing that, on the ultimate scale of life, these are not so important. We can come together as people, families, neighborhoods, towns, cities, and states, and as one nation under God with liberty and justice for all.

We can say prayers for the people killed and injured, and especially for their families. We can pray for the safety of the rescue workers and that they, too, will heal from this awful ordeal. We can give blood, money, and supplies to the cause. We can, each in our own way, do whatever we can. Now is a time of unity and coming together as a people. These things we can do.

Make no mistake, justice will be served. Our leaders will do their job, as difficult as it is. We will come out the other side of this tragedy stronger than ever as a people.

My heart and prayers and those of my family go out to all of the people who have been affected by this tragedy. May God watch over you all and bring you comfort in your time of need.

And the Wisdom to know the difference

The wisdom here is in knowing that we cannot undo what has happened. We can, however, make sure these poor souls did not die in vain. We must treat this awful event as a lesson, a lesson that our world is in desperate need of healing. We must use this event as a "wake-up call" to bring peace and healing to our fragile planet.

Yes, we must rid our world of terrorists and anyone who would empower them. This is essential if we are to ever live in peace again. However, in the end, we must unite with all the good people on this planet, whatever their race or religion, to bring an end to this senseless violence. We must, beginning now, envision world peace for ourselves and for future generations.

5

Letters and Prayers:
To Heal A Nation

*"I find the great thing in this world is not so much where
we stand, as in what direction we are moving. To reach the
port of heaven, we must sail sometimes with the wind and
sometimes against it—but we must sail, and not drift, nor lie
at anchor."*

— *Oliver Wendell Holmes*

Letter to an Innocent

By Sue Shackles, MW
Washington State, USA

D^{ear} Juliana,

We didn't know each other, as we lived on opposite sides of the country. Our paths may never have crossed, and I might have lived my life in ignorance of your existence. All of that changed on the morning of September 11, 2001.

I wonder how you felt as you and your mother boarded the plane that day. I'd guess you were excited at the prospect of going to Los Angeles. I've traveled with young ones, and I know how bubbly you must have felt in the face of this great adventure. Your mother was probably a little worried about how you would react, wondering whether boredom would strike you before you reached your destination and whether you would behave yourself well.

Did relatives come to see you leave? Did you give big hugs and kisses and wave as you started down that tunnel into the body of the plane? I bet you were all smiles for the stewardess as she pointed out your seat. Maybe you were given coloring books and crayons to play with while the plane filled up and people pushed by you. Were you in the window seat? Did you look outside as you wiggled in anticipation, waiting for the moment the engines would start? I hope you enjoyed your peanuts. Were they yummy? Sometimes you have to be careful, 'cause those bags can split easily and you lose them on the floor. I hope that didn't happen to you. It's important that you were having fun.

Who was more scared when the plane started to move? Was it you or your mom? It's my least favorite part of the whole journey, and I always hold my children's hands tight, even though it doesn't scare them at all. Did your mommy hold your hand?

When you were up in the air and the nice stewardess was bringing you something to drink, did you have Sprite or Coke? Sprite's my favorite, even though the bubbles go up my nose. If you brought a friend along, some special doll or teddy bear, I hope that you shared, 'cause teddies get thirsty, too, you know.

Did you notice what was happening with the bad people at first or were you too interested in the things that four-year-old little girls like to do? You must have noticed the yelling and your mommy getting worried. Little girls know these things without being told, no matter how much mommies try to hide it from them. I bet she tried to shield your view of the bad things and distract you with something else. That's what mommies who love their children do. You must have been afraid, though, and asked her what was going on. You were old enough to realize that these things weren't normal.

The plane made a big turn, didn't it? Did you see the wing of the plane disappear out of the window? It always scares me when that happens, because I'm afraid the plane is going to crash. Did I tell you I'm a big old scaredy cat? Your mommy's talking to you, but you can't really hear what she's saying because there are lots of other people making noise in the plane and it hurts your ears. It's okay, Sweetheart. She's not saying anything that would make any sense to you anyway. She's trying to fill your mind with nonsense talk to shut out the sound of fear that is echoing through the body of the plane. Let her fasten your seatbelt again, even though she's pulling it too tight. She's trying to protect you in the only way she knows how. You can't see inside her head or her heart, but she's dying inside, full of guilt and pain for subjecting you to this. See, your mommy would run into a burning building to save you. She would give up her own life. The last thing she ever expected to happen was to be strapped helpless and powerless in the seat beside you, unable to save either one of you from what was going to happen.

I know that in those final moments, as the buildings in front of you grew closer and closer, that she must have pulled your head close to her chest, away from the terrible sight looming in the window. I know, because I'm a mommy too, and that's what I would have done. I'm sure that you felt her face against your hair, her kisses and tears falling onto you like rain. You heard her heart beating so hard it sounded like it was going to leap out of her chest.

And then you felt nothing; you saw nothing; you heard nothing. At least, that's my prayer for you, because no little four-year-old girl should have to be aware of that. I pray that the impact killed you instantly and you were not aware of the blast or the fire.

I never knew you, little Juliana, but in a sense I did. You're every little four-year-old girl who ever lived. You had the same dreams, the same potential. Did the cure for cancer or AIDS die along with you? Could you have been the first woman president? We'll never know. Your tiny life was snuffed out in a game of chess you didn't even realize you were a part of. I grieve for you as though you were my own. All of the mothers in the world grieve for you, as we know only too well how many times we have boarded planes with our own children. How easily you could have been our baby. Sleep well, precious one.

Love, A mommy.

Note: The little girl to whom this letter is addressed is Juliana Valentine McCourt, who was a passenger on Flight 175...the one that struck the second tower.

Dear Jamie

By Trina Lambert
Colorado, USA

Jamie was a 10-year-old from far away, almost foreign to me, New Jersey. I was a 10-year-old from windswept western Nebraska. I chose her name from the pen pal list because I hoped she might be a boy. Although I went by Patrina, I introduced myself as Pat—so I might appear to be a boy, too. In her next letter, she mentioned that a lot of girls had written her, thinking she was a boy. I remained silent—and continued to sign my name as Pat. Did I ever confess my initial intentions? I can't remember.

What I do remember is that we shared stories about our Christmas celebrations and school activities. She told me when she received her saint name. I discussed the difference in confirmation for Lutherans. We grew older. Although busy girls, we never stopped writing.

She joined ROTC as she started college. I attended college in Ohio, closer to her than in Nebraska, but still so very far away from New Jersey. After graduation, I moved further west to Denver, and she began her military career. The closest she came to being in the west was while stationed in Ft. Sill, Oklahoma.

Our letter writing tapered, but we remained on each other's Christmas card lists. I married and had kids, while she stayed single and moved up the ranks in the military. Her last card with any real information came to me in 1997 or 1998. She sent me her business card from her job in the Pentagon. I haven't heard from her since, but my Christmas letters have not been returned from her Arlington, Virginia address.

My first email to her on September 11 was returned promptly—no doubt her rank has changed and so has her work e-mail address. Next, I "Googled" her. I may have found her home email address. I have written, but still no reply has come.

What else did Google tell me? Only that she has become a serious runner like I was so many years ago in high school. In three years, her 5K times have improved by six minutes. At 39, she must be more fit than she has been in years. Surely, she will run again.

And yet, I hear the Army has the most casualties in the Pentagon tragedy. I pray that I will not see her picture in a newspaper in the days ahead. As I write, I glance at her 9th and 10th grade school photos, look at her thick, shiny hair and her dark, prominent eyes, and I begin to think I cannot pray enough for her. I read the back of the photo where she wrote, "Maybe someday we'll meet." Maybe.

Why do people who belong to some long forgotten period of our lives still matter to us? Jamie and I never did meet, yet I worry for her safety. Is this a selfless concern for her mortality or does her existence prove that I, too, still exist? Could we renew our friendship, or was our letter writing from a time before we knew what we might become and who we really were? Can an at-home mom and a career military woman really have anything in common, or is what we already shared all we'll ever have?

I'd like to have the chance to find out. I'd like to know that we still have a someday in our future, that this will be the start of a reconnection, that I won't take for granted that this person from my past still exists, and that from the rubble of a national tragedy, our friendship will be more than it used to be. And so I say her name aloud in church, I add her name to online prayers, and on the back steps of my house, I break down in a plea to God.

Within a couple hours, the list of missing shows up on my computer screen. So many names...those of colleagues maybe, but not hers. I start a letter like so many others I have written before. "Dear Jamie," and yet I can only write a couple paragraphs, brief in my thankfulness for her safety. How do I catch up on her current life when the nation's current events are still so huge? Most certainly, her military work is just beginning.

I send my email to the new address and wait.

Special Days

By Shannon Walker
Florida, USA

It has almost been a year since our nation's tragedy on September 11, 2001. We have all, in some way, offered a helping hand and a prayer to those suffering the loss of loved ones. Some of us sent donations, while others wrote letters or offered hours of work to help regain composure in our great state of New York. I do not think a day goes by that we don't stop and say a prayer, remembering the homes that will forever be changed by the huge loss. We've heard many stories about how lives were lost or forever altered on that day, and for every terrible story we've heard, there are thousands of others that, although not quite as tragic, are sad just the same—people whose special days and memories will be forever marred.

My father-in-law, Bill, woke up that morning planning to celebrate his birthday. He walked outside to get his paper, and a neighbor advised him to turn on his TV. The horrible images on his television told him that he would never forget this birthday! I remember so clearly talking with him on the phone. He said, "I feel guilty even mentioning it, but I don't know how I'll ever feel okay to smile or celebrate on this day again."

I felt an overwhelming sorrow, and I tried to find some words of comfort to offer him—but they would not come. I thought of my little girl who had celebrated her birthday just two days earlier. A feeling of sadness came over me, as my mind was flooded with "what if's."

What if it had happened on her special day? Would people look down on us if we celebrated? What words of comfort could I have given her to let her know it is okay to celebrate your special day without feelings of guilt and confusion?

I'm not an expert on advice—I can only say what is in my heart. That day will always weigh heavily on our hearts as a day of great loss. But it should not stop us from living. Stop and remember, say a prayer for our nation, and then rejoice on your special day. Celebrate your anniversary or birthday or the birthday of a loved one. Though it is a tragic date in history, it's still a special day to you and your loved ones. Those horrible people took enough from us on September 11, 2001—let's not allow them to take another ounce of joy from us. Though we will never forget, we must move forward and continue our pursuit of happiness with the reassurance that it is still okay to smile.

My Dear American

By Kathy Cyr
Connecticut, USA

Ⓜy Dear American,

I had a revelation today, and I would like to share it with you in hopes of gaining your forgiveness.

At times in my life I have taken you for granted, never appreciating the little things you do. I have taken the words you speak and twisted them around, only hearing what I wish to hear, never fully understanding your depth.

I have looked at the color of your skin and judged you. I have criticized your way of life and your religion. I have criticized and judged you for being who you are.

I have hatefully envied you for your wealth, your material things, and your riches in family togetherness. I have turned a deaf ear when you were in need. I have looked the other way when you needed my help. I turned my back when you reached out for me.

I have given my life precedence over yours. I have made my concerns, my feelings, and my way of thinking matter far more than you. Words can never really express all the mixed emotions I feel for you at this moment. For you see, I was wrong.

It has taken a tragedy to open my eyes to all the beauty you hold. I see now that you are the better person. I see now that your differences are what make you special. I have believed you to be weak and shallow minded, when in truth you are stronger and more giving than I am.

How could I have been so blind for so long?

I see your image flash before me standing tall and straight against the enemy. I see your tears and know your heart is breaking for the lost souls and those that have passed on. I watch with intensity and feel as though I am dying a slow death inside.

I want to reach for you, hold you, and tell you everything will be all right. I want to wipe away the tears. But I cannot, so here I sit, my Dear American, trying to find the right words to bring back the peace and joy you once felt.

I make these promises to you on this day, my Dear American. I shall forever hold you close within my heart. Your children will be loved and protected as though they were my own. You shall have my utmost respect and my gratitude for being a better human being than I ever could. It shall be my honor and a privilege to stand by your side in unity.

Nevermore will my feelings waiver. My heart is open—my arms are outstretched—reach for me. I am here.

Grieve, America

By Raynette Eitel
Nevada, USA

Grieve, America.
　　Pull the black silk of night
　　Tight about your body
　　And fill it with your tears.

Mourn, America,
Even as you long for sleep
To fill all the dark corners
Of your dreams with healing light.

Have Courage, America,
As you press your face
Against the window of tomorrow,
Too afraid to look.

Rage, America,
Howl your anger
Across the rubble like a wounded wolf,
Then carry that rage as a torch
Into secret caves where evil hides.

Hope, America,
Stars and stripes binding us together,
Lips moving in prayer,

Arms outstretched, palms up,
To catch the rainbow
As it comes.

A Letter to My Children

By Crystel Riggs
South Carolina, USA

We started the day just as we do every day. Somehow, in spite of all the planning, the morning ended, as they all seem to, in a mad dash to make it to school on time. We did not want to be late on this particular morning, because our Governor was scheduled to appear at the school for a special program, after which he would make a long walk through the city. It had been widely publicized and was to be a major event.

I saw the Governor before I left the school. He walked down the halls of the building, admiring the artwork each class had posted on bulletin boards outside their rooms. He would occasionally stop to admire a particular piece of work and smile. Instead of his usual suit, he was wearing clothes more suited for the long walk that was scheduled. Sneakers, running pants, and a t-shirt made him look much like any other parent in the school.

I had only been home for a little while when your Dad called asking me to turn on the TV to see what I could find out about the plane crash. He had heard something about an accident on the radio, but his reception was bad and he couldn't hear it all. When I turned the television on, I could see the tower of the World Trade Center with smoke rolling out of it. As the commentators discussed the horrible accident, another plane approached, and before the world, it made a sharp turn and crashed into the second building.

It didn't register at that moment what I was seeing. At first I believed it was a replay of the crash, but the building was already on fire when I saw the plane hit. It struck me then that I was watching something as it happened. I was witnessing an attack on our country. I sat down and tried to make sense of what I was watching as the television continued to replay the scene. Reports were coming in so fast—reports of hijacked planes that had taken off just a while earlier, a plane crashing into the pentagon, another plane missing and full of people. There were people on those planes, people in the buildings…children, moms and dads, grandparents, brothers, and sisters. My mind raced to piece together the bits and pieces, and I realized that I had just watched people—probably thousands of people, die.

It was devastating to make that connection. Time was passing quickly, and it seemed that each minute or two unveiled a view of evil from a different angle. My heart ached. Fear and panic gripped me as I sat wondering what more was to come. It wasn't even 9:30 a.m. yet. Before the day was half over, I had seen more death and felt more fear than my entire life's worth of experience could ever have prepared me for.

It was just after lunch when our Governor appeared on television. He had been taken back to the state's capital immediately following the news of the attack. The walk he had planned through our town had been cancelled. His walking attire had been exchanged for a suit, and he looked more like a leader now than a parent. Our state was placed on the highest level of alert, and the Governor explained what this meant to us here in South Carolina. Many businesses were closing, all government buildings were locked down, and schools were dismissing classes. I kept a constant vigil at the television, watching to see if your school would be closed while I kept telling myself you'd be safe there and wouldn't have to watch me fall apart in front of the television. I would not be able to explain what was happening to any of you. I didn't understand it myself.

Today marks two weeks since the day of the attack. There are reports in the news of biological weapons and the possibilities of such attacks. Security issues about the nuclear plant near our home are oftentimes mentioned on the radio and TV news. Just a couple of days ago, your Dad and I sat down together and planned what we would do in the event of an attack on the nuclear plant. Two weeks ago, I was not aware of which buildings in town were built with bomb shelters—today I am. Now I wake up apprehensive about turning on the news to see what is happening in our world. There is such uncertainty about what each new day might bring. Sending all of you off to school every morning is not easy. I worry that I may not be able to get to you fast enough if I should need to. I worry about you being away from me, and about who will protect you while I am not there. Two weeks ago, I would have considered these feelings irrational or silly—today I don't.

So many people left home that morning with plans to see their families and children again, but they never will. There were hundreds who went into those buildings to save people, and they, too, were lost when the buildings collapsed. So many people watched it as it happened...terror unfolding—evil coming to life—taking life. All over the world candles burn, people pray, memorials stand, and flags fly. Right now, we are still in the middle of it. The threat of war looms large and emotions run deep. There are things we need to keep from happening, but there are still other things that we need to make sure will last.

We should never forget that some people don't need a good reason to have a reason for what they do—there is such a thing as pure evil. Nothing we can do in our lives will keep us from harm all the time; we are not guaranteed a tomorrow. Knowing this, we should never treat anyone cold-heartedly, because we never know what kind of pain they suffer inside of their own hearts. To add to anyone's pain would be a bad thing to do, and so many in the world are now left with a pain that will never go away. We need to be sure to treat all people fairly, respectfully, and gently. Never leave someone you love without saying "I love you." Sometimes there are no other opportunities. Be happy with what you have in your life rather than complaining about what you don't. Remember that if everything was lost—the things we'd wish for most deeply would be those we love and who love us.

It will be years before you read this letter, but it needs to be written now—while it's fresh. We, as humans, have a way of forgetting. Our mind, with its amazing abilities, tends to diminish, cover up, and lighten memories to help us cope with certain events. While it is true that this is a helpful and sometimes necessary step in moving on, there are those occasions when the severity of a particular circumstance needs to be remembered. We've seen our President brought to tears. We have been shown the faces and told stories of those lost. We've watched as all across the world, other nations mourn with us. We've been forced to face a reality that most of us would never have considered a possibility. This, we must remember.

I love you,
Mom

AMEN

By Karen Hawkins
Maine, USA

He shed a tear today—
One tear for every soul.
And it poured...
Washing away the darkness,
Making the way for light and love,
As we pray together—
Each in our own way
For healing.
Amen.
God Bless Us All.

Thy Rod and Thy Staff, They Comfort Me

By Margaret Byers Smith, Ph.D.
Arkansas, USA

I scooted my chair closer to the computer, watching the update on September 11 as the news flashed across my screen. My fingers froze on the keyboard as images unfurled themselves within my mind.

First, I vaguely remembered Pearl Harbor and hurriedly breathed a prayer that this was not another Pearl Harbor, that horrible Day of Infamy. I am sure that, as a preschooler, I didn't understand the meaning of Pearl Harbor until the black out curtains, ration stamps, and gold stars began to appear. I vomited every day on the way to school.

My eyes still clouded with memory, the images quickly flashed to FDR's death and that sad trip cross-country. Because of that, I can't even hum *Going Home* without tears in my eyes.

Immediately my mind turned to the rest of WWII, especially the memory of the day the dynamite plant where my Dad was working in the Bay Area of San Francisco, California, blew up. I remembered being glued to the short wave radio we had as they announced the explosion, the police work, the bodies. I remembered Mom praying and our running to hug Dad when he walked through the door safe. Something had told him to walk outside instead of staying on his duty station. If he had stayed, he would have been among the dead. Tears again.

My memory cogs moved promptly forward to hearing about Sputnik on the radio. I had a tiny baby and was still in my teens. I had to pray because we did not know how the Cold War was going to change because of this. I figured out evacuation plans to keep my child safe.

Then I remembered being in my home, now in San Diego, and hearing an odd droning noise. I went outside, looked up, and saw the sky filled with planes. No explanation and nothing to do but pray. Later we found it was the Strategic Air Command scrambling because of the Cuban Missile Crisis.

I remembered the day when I was so poor and young with my child that I did not have a television. The neighbor later banging frantically on my door and said, "I thought you would like to know—the President is dead." He meant President Kennedy. When he left, I turned on the radio, collapsed to my knees, cried, and prayed, but the country went on.

Robert Kennedy fell not soon afterwards, and it seemed there were assassinations all the time. But our country went on.

I remembered the day I was out on beautiful Point Loma on the Cal Western College campus when other students ran up to me saying, "They are killing students now." It was the Kent State slaying. I had no tears left for our beautiful country by then.

Other tragedies have come and gone, and I met them stoically with prayers—until the shootings at the various schools across the nation. I was living in Arkansas during the Jonesboro, Arkansas, shooting and got that news from my computer news service. How I wept and cried for our country that day and for each subsequent shooting.

Then September 11. Another day of infamy. I froze, shocked, at the computer and thought, *Lord, I am too old to sit and worry about this one. Please don't let it be another Pearl Harbor. Bless our nation and keep my loved ones safe. Thy will be done.* I did call my daughter in the bay area of California at Stanford University, and she told me the steps she had taken for safety. So I decided to leave it in the Lord's hands and not follow the news glued to the television set. I emailed my husband that our daughter was safe and taking care, and then I calmly set about my other computer tasks, as I am homebound and that is my usual routine.

Every day since I have prayed for our nation—and for its and my loved ones' safety.

It was much later when I found out that I, indeed, had loved ones and friends at the site in D.C. or very close. Every one of them was safe. My prayers were answered once again, like they always are. Sometimes the answer is "no," but I have been blessed with so many "yes" answers that I have come to depend on them and feel no fear. Thy rod and thy staff, they comfort me.

God Cries for ALL of Us

By V. K. Mullins
Michigan, USA

God Cries for all of us.
As the rains poured down
upon the earth last night,
God wept.
Not for those taken,
for they are with Him,
but for those of us
left behind.
God bless us all.

Remember Those Who Died

By Bea Sheftel
Connecticut, USA

L et us remember those who have died. Let us pray for them, their families, and our country. All our problems seem very minor compared to what these people suffered and what their families are suffering.

These are notes I've taken watching TV and the *Oprah* show. I hope they give you a measure of comfort.

Diane Sawyer said, "We are suffering from wounded numbness."

September 14, five men were pulled alive from the rubble of the Twin Towers.

There are many stories of bravery. First and foremost are the rescue workers who go beyond the call of duty. They are very special people.

One man was walking down to safety when an associate had a heart attack. He went back to help the man and now is among the dead.

Many men and women were able to call their families and leave messages of love. This shows what is most important in all our lives—it is not our jobs, how much money we have, or anything else, but love.

The Franciscan Priest who was Chaplin of the Fire Department died as he leaned over a dying man praying the last Rites. He left this earth with the name of Jesus on his lips.

An entire young family in Easton, Connecticut, was killed when their plane was crashed into the Twin Towers. Mother, father, and baby all died together.

Another man, who would have been safe, returned to his office to stay by the side of his lifelong friend who was a paraplegic. No greater love has any man than to lay down his life for another.

Each story is unique and tragic, and yet through the horror, we see real heroes and heroines who helped others at the risk of peril to their own lives.

It is said that when even evil exists, goodness abounds even more. We certainly have seen this in the stories coming out of this terrorist act.

Dr. Phil McGraw on *Oprah* said we are all a family. We need to grieve even if we didn't know anyone personally who was hurt or killed at the Twin Towers. We have all lost someone—many someones—and we have a right to grieve.

No person should feel insignificant. We are all important—to ourselves, our families, and our country.

God bless the rescue workers. God bless those who died. God bless the families.

God bless our country.

Goodbye, Lost Ones, Goodbye

By Jennifer LB Leese
Maryland, USA

A flash, an explosion, a blast and flames
　What just happened in the sky?
Shock, distress, fright, and horror
Everything has gone awry.
Chaos, panic, dismay, and turmoil
Who planned this disaster and why?
Scream, cry, wail, and shout
Why do people have to die?
Sadness, misery, grief, and anguish
Everything is so dry.
Disgust, anger, hatred, and rage
Selfish ones took over the sky.
Darkness, torment, tragedy, and pain
Our lives have changed, we cannot deny.
Despair, mourning, sorrow, and agony
Goodbye, lost ones, goodbye.

"Where Were You, God?"

By Dave Koy
Wisconsin, USA

Newspaper headlines on September 11 screamed the terrifying news: AMERICA UNDER ATTACK! The unthinkable had happened. Terrorists hijacked four commercial airliners and in a bizarre suicide pact crashed all four planes, two of them into the World Trade Center and one into the Pentagon. The fourth crashed in rural Pennsylvania. Thousands died. The entire world gasped. And our nation mourned.

People rushed to their churches, mosques, and temples to pray and to wonder, *"God, where were you? How could you allow this to happen?"* There are those who say the carnage of September 11 was a punishment from God for our nation's sinful ways. Personally, I believe it was the evil in the hearts of the terrorists who perpetrated this horrific deed. One of the privileges we enjoy as citizens of this world is our God given free will. It is our choice to do good or evil, to obey God or shun His commands.

Unfortunately, the United States as a nation, like so many other nations, has chosen to disobey God's authority and His laws. We continue to find new ways to break God's commandments— new measures to push His hand of protection and blessing further from our presence.

A few days after the terrorist attacks, Ann Graham Lutz, popular speaker, author, and daughter of evangelist Billy Graham, appeared on television's 700 Club. She was asked to comment on the terrible tragedy of September 11. "We have told God to get out of our public schools, get out of our government buildings, get out of our public places," said Lutz. "We have repeatedly told God to get out of our public lives, period. And then we ask where God is in our time of need."

And she is right. For the past 40 years groups like the ACLU and many liberal judges have fed us the lie of "separation of church and state," and we have swallowed every spoonful. We have been told God belongs in our homes and our churches, but not in the public square. We have been ordered to remove nativity scenes from public places, Bibles and prayers from public schools, crosses from cemeteries and the Ten Commandments from government buildings. Contrary to what our Founding Fathers felt about God's supreme authority, we have been told America doesn't need God.

But when something terrible happens in a public place, like it did at Columbine, like it did in Oklahoma City, and like it did on September 11, we quickly ask, "God, where were you?"

Our nation will shed a torrent of tears in the weeks and months ahead. And our Creator no doubt will weep right along with us. He understands the pain we feel; He knows the trials and challenges that lay ahead. But there is hope. The Bible in Romans 8:28 reminds us that, *"...in all things God works for the good of those who love Him, who have been called according to His purpose."* The God of our universe can help heal our wounds and comfort our aching hearts—if we will let Him.

All across the American landscape we see signs that say, *"God Bless America."* I truly hope this is more than just another catchy phrase plastered on a billboard, marquee, or sign post to make us feel better. I truly hope we are ready to return God's influence to all segments of our life—both private and public.

As we rebuild our nation from the rubble of the terrorist attacks, are we truly ready and willing to blend God's authority into the brick and mortar, the sweat and tears of our new America? Or will we wait until the next catastrophe and once again ask: "God, where were You?"

On Bended Knee

By Cathy Laska
Wisconsin,USA

To the brave and strong of that dreadful September day,
Who would have thought death in such a cruel way.

The men and women who gave their lives,
The innocent, the young, the old, the wise.

Explosions, screams, buildings crashing at horrific speeds,
Hearts once turned inward, now, turned towards others needs.

Intertwined in the agony and strife,
Friends and strangers rush to their neighbors plight.

People embracing one another,
Panic and running to take safe cover.

Others scurry through the streets to flee,
For one time only, some run to church falling on bended knee.

Thank you to all who gave their life,
Thank you to those protecting our skies day and night.

Thank you to those who fight this war overseas,

OH, LORD, FORGIVE THIS NATION,
KEEP US ON BENDED KNEE.

6

Voices of America's Children

"Train a child in the way he should go and when he is old, he will not turn from it."

— *The Bible*
Proverbs 22:6

Not Just a Promise

By Rob Shoemaker
Age 6
North Carolina, USA

We were there when it happened. We watched it on TV. It was probably really bad to be there. I help my Mom light a candle every night, and she says it helps people remember how bad it was. I promise, I'll never forget.

Sorry

By Jolene Plummer
Age 7
Wisconsin, USA

On September 11, 2001, I feel sorry for the families of the people who passed away.

The War

MyKaela Korryn Edrich
Age 7
Wisconsin, USA

This one man wanted to kill everybody, and he crashed a plane into a big building. The airplane hit the building and broke through the building. The building fell down, and the humans tried to run out, but half of them died.

A plane crashed by our house. We lived in Indiana, Pennsylvania, and I saw the plane crash into the ground on TV. A man fought the bad guys and the plane crashed into the ground.

It was a war because the people were fighting each other. I got scared and wanted my father to buy some guns. So we went to Wal-Mart to look at the guns, but my mom said we couldn't buy them. So I asked if we could buy a bow and arrow. My mom said no because it was not good for kids.

The planes crashing scared me. It made me feel like we should get out of this place. I was scared because I thought that maybe one of us would die. I thought that moving to another place would keep us safe.

I think that people should not make a war. I think they should have stopped the war.

From Tears to Smiles

By Jade Alana Walker
Age 8
Florida, USA

On September 9, we were celebrating my 8th birthday, and two days later, on my Grandpa's birthday, men went to an airport and robbed a plane and on purpose crashed into the biggest building in the world. They killed their selves and people in the building and people on the plane.

I really felt worried because my Aunt Heidi lives in New York and might have got hurt. I feel bad for the people who died and I also feel sorry for my Grandpa—because every year on his birthday he will think of that horrible day.

All you good citizens out there—keep smiling.

Silence and Sacrifice

By Alfonso Reyes
Age 9
Arizona, USA

We lack peace
While evil screams
We treasure memories
Through our tears
We seek the truth
And the lost power.
Peace needs silence
While terror screams
We pray tears
And the respect and trust
We all need.
Power we seek through the end.
Treasure we seek through
The great night moon.
Meanwhile, the dark clouds
Are heading this way
To destroy peace
All over the earth.
Our tears glow
At midnight
While the coyotes howl
At the great glowing moon

The September 11th Tragedy

By Katarina Beth Miller
Age 9
Wisconsin, USA

On September 11, I was in the dentist's office, and I heard about the two twin Towers knocked down by a plane. But I thought it was just two small buildings. But then my teacher, Scott Johnson, told me when I got back—he asked if I knew anything about the Twin Towers, and I said, "yes," and he said the class didn't know anything about it and he was going to turn on the news to show everybody. He did and everybody was surprised.

But a couple of days after that everyone kept talking about it and my Mom kept watching the news. The day we heard about Osama bin Laden and what he had done was something no one could forget.

How I felt that day was kind of weird because when it happened, I thought it wasn't a big deal, but when I got to school, it was a big deal to everyone when they heard about it. But when we saw people trying to jump out windows to save their lives, it was sad, and more than 1,000 people died on September 11—even on some people's birthdays.

It was a tragedy. I am happy and sad—I am happy because they went to heaven, and I am sad because they died and had to jump out a window to try to survive, and I feel bad. I wish September 11 would not have happened at all. Osama bin Laden should be sorry for killing a lot of New York and killing people on the plane that day.

Terrorists Attack the U.S.

By Jared Amor
Age 10
California, USA

The drivers of the two airplanes were the terrorists. They died when they went into the Trade Centers. The Trade Centers collapsed. New York is in smoke. My Mom's friend's brother was in the hijacked plane that hit the second Tower. When the planes hit, they got halfway through, then blew up.

My Aunt is going to take pictures of the fallen Trade Centers for me. The Trade Centers were the most important to New York. The terrorists also destroyed the Pentagon. That was also the important thing to the United States. My Aunt saw everything that the terrorists did to New York. This is history.

Terrorists can be 20 to 100 people. Parents in New York and Washington took their kids out of school because of what had happened. And just in case the terrorists attack the schools. A couple of years ago terrorists killed over 200 kids in the Oklahoma Bombing.

President Bush asked if we would pray, and he said thanks to all the people who gave blood.

Terrorist Attacks

By Turner Benard
Age 10
Louisiana, USA

I think the attacks were very well thought out. Whoever did this should have aimed at least at something military and not at innocent people. I think they should construct a fake Air Force 1 and advertise where the fake is going and then send the President far away from that location. I think it is sick that they killed all of those innocent people! I have been praying every night for them. I think that this will go on into social studies books in about two years. This is the first attack ever on the mainland of America—the United States! The planes that crashed into the World Trade Center were the worst of the crashes. I think that attack just silhouetted what they really wanted to do to us. I hope that whoever did it should get exactly what they deserve.

I think they should give airplane pilots weapons so they can defend themselves against hijackers. What they did was just horrible. Personally, it makes me very mad and so sad.

Did you know that three Poboy shops here, run by people from Afghanistan, were harassed so much they had to close their shops? *Shameful.*

I think that we will eventually catch whoever was behind this attack. I think Bin Laden was behind the terrorist attacks. I think it will take at least two months to catch who did it.

The people who are hiding him, once they see what will happen to them, they will give him up as if it were nothing.

A memorial service in Central Park is being held on September 23 for all of the firemen who lost their lives in the attack. Whoever harbors the terrorists should get the same punishment as the terrorists themselves.

I really hope they catch Bin Laden because I think he was behind this all. They should just allow commercial flights carrying mail to fly. I really feel sorry for any families that lost someone. I think God is very, very sad about what happened.

God probably wants us to pray very hard for everyone in this ordeal. The terrorists probably weren't thinking of God's Golden Rule when they killed our people. They'll sure be sad when they have to come before God.

The Twin Towers

By Moslin Cruz
Age 10
Arizona, USA

Together in sadness
Tragedy
Through time
Violence bothers
Our happiness
Enemy terror
Can make us stronger
Our symbols are
In trustworthy hands
Memories will
Bless our endurance.

When You're Ready

By Cody Shoemaker
Age 11
North Carolina, USA

I don't know your names, but I know that you are very sad and scared because you have lost someone you love. How do I know this? I know because my Mom is sad and started crying when she tried to explain to me what happened at the World Trade Center in New York; at the Pentagon in Arlington, Virginia; and in Pennsylvania. My Mom is a very great lady and she wouldn't be so sad if she didn't feel someone else was sad and hurt. So that's how I know.

Maybe you can't read this right now, but after a while, you will be able to. Right now, you are hurt and you are scared. But I want you to know that I am hurt and scared for you. The moms, dads, brothers, sisters, sons, daughters, cousins, uncles, aunts, and friends who were there when this awful thing happened are still with us. They are in our hearts and in our memories and as long as we keep remembering them, they will live forever.

The whole country and the whole world have come together and are crying with each one of you who lost someone on September 11, 2001. We won't let you go through this alone because now, we are all one great big family.

So when you can wipe away the tears and read this, you'll know how much we love and care for all of you, all of those who died or are lost, and all those who have not stopped working since the whole thing started. I'm not telling you not to be sad, because I know this is a very hard thing to go through. But I am telling you that you don't have to be sad alone. The whole world is sad with you.

What Happened in Sadness

By Jennifer Cruz
Age 11
Arizona, USA

What happened in sadness
Families lost
Never able to be whole again
Feeling sad
In this lifetime
They could not say goodbye

The September 11 Twin Towers Crash

Brianna Hardy
Age 11
Wisconsin, USA

On September 11, I was at Kate Goodrich Elementary School and all the fifth grade classes had to see a school puppet show. It was about how people felt, and when the puppet show was over, some people in fifth grade had to go to their classes. I had to go to Social Studies class. Mrs. Monti turned on the TV on the news. I saw planes crashed into the twin towers.

I felt real sad that Osama bin Laden killed half of New York. I wish that Osama bin Laden would never have crashed into the twin tower, and I cried when I got home because soon it will be Christmas. I felt mad the kids moms and dads died and they will not have a good Christmas because their mom and dad died. If I was in their position, I would feel mad, too.

I am sorry, New York.

Helpless

By Amy Shackles
Age 12
Washington State, USA

The date is the 19th of September, 2001—just eight days since the catastrophe of the 11th. A plane ran into the Twin Towers. I can still recall where I was when I found out. I was at my best friend's house. We were getting ready to go to school. I thought it was a joke at first, you know? The tricks that people play sometimes? Well...it turns out, it wasn't. It was real, and I couldn't do anything to stop it from happening, though I wish I could.

We talked about it a lot in social studies class, and I talked about it a lot at a bingo site, where my friends and I talked. I'm still getting over the shock that somebody could do something like that. There are kids without parents, other people without aunts, uncles, nephews, nieces, daughters, sons, grandparents, or friends. I don't like killing...I like stories about killing, and drama, and suspense, but this was real life! No way am I going to be the same, but like I said I had a small taste of that disaster, because I was lucky enough not to have anyone anywhere near New York state. I felt very bad for the people who suffered, and still do. To those of you who had relatives of friends in that crash, I am so sorry. The least I can do is say something so...God Bless You! I really hope you think I put an effort into helping you, but do not turn to destruction of our fellow man. If we do, we're just saying, "We're just like you." So when you read this, be of good heart. I may be only 12, but it's not age that matters, it's knowledge that counts.

Angels

By Giovanni Aponte
Age 12
Florida, USA

Angels, angels, angels,
they are all around us.
They are in the big, blue sky.
On the day a big plane came rushing through
the Twin Towers,
some people say there were angels around us.
Angels were watching the people
while they ran down the stairs.
Angels were watching the people who were first found.
The Twin Towers almost came down in 1993.
I saw it on TV.
That day, I could see angels holding the Twin Towers down,
but on September 11, 2001,
maybe the angels were saving the people they could,
and the Twin Towers came crashing down.
Angels, angels, angels were all around.

United We Stand

By Maureen Gard
Age 13
Illinois, USA

Lady Liberty looked over her nation with pride shining in
her eyes,
When she saw a plane fly over the horizon, with chilling
screams and cries.
In a burst of flame and smoke so black that it seemed like
night had come,
As the plane crashed into the tower of the World Trade Center
and the many cries became none.

More cries of pain and fear echoed through the streets,
As people jumped out of windows, fire covered them like
sheets.
The thump of a body, the cry of the dead,
The screams for the missing, the crack of a head.

Another plane appears out of the blue,
And into the second tower it flew.
More fire and screams and smoke of black night,
As all for their lives began to fight.

News had come that the Pentagon was ablaze,
And above the building rose an evil haze.
First fell the one tower and then number two,
And all around the city, dust and debris flew.

Many were missing, police and firefighters alike,
Soon the rescue workers began their hike.
They climbed up the rubble, hoping existence would still
shine,
But for every life found, blood was uncovered like spilled red
wine.

"Why…Why?" many screamed, as loved ones were missing,
While in other countries their happy laughter sounded like evil
hissing.
That was when the fourth plane crashed into an open field,
And when many lives began to yield.

Children were getting out of school and finding out about the
attack,
Some were so numb that when watching the news they were
taken aback.
More questions rose and so did the sorrow,
People came out to give and their expertise to borrow.

The evil behind this bloody event had hoped to hear "We give
up" at call,
But sadly to them we yelled "United We Stand, Divided We
Fall!"
And so we came together, with pride glowing from each face,
As red, white, and blue colors flew around the country like
beautiful lace.

Freedom rings across the land and justice shall prevail,
And prayers were sent to God with love and many began to
hail.
Fists thrown into the air with shouts of USA,
From all the prairies to the ocean bays!

So here we stand today, now stronger then before,
And Lady Liberty continues to watch us with love and adore.

Dedicated to every person in the country, for everyone was
affected on the date of 9/11/01

I Think Americans Should Show Patriotism

By Jeremy Pedelose
Age 13
Florida, USA

I think Americans should show patriotism for the United States of America. The way we helped each other when the Twin Towers were attacked showed patriotism. The most moving thing I have ever seen was the true spirit of patriotism then, and it can't be displayed enough throughout our country. Patriotism is all about the way you act when your country is attacked by terrorists or other countries.

I think that the people of the United States are clinging together showing their patriotism since September 11. We are stronger than ever, and we will defend our country, and we will never give up on Old Glory. We will never be touched if we all work together as one country instead of pointing fingers. Sometimes, it takes a tragedy to bring people and families together, and what was meant to divide us, united us.

I think the patriots who helped did the best thing they could trying to save the victims on September 11, and they are the real patriots in the United States. All the friends, family members, rescuers, policemen, and firefighters who lost their lives that morning should never be forgotten as long as Old Glory waves. Countries that have soldiers are countries that have lots of patriots on their side. We are AmeriCANS, not AmeriCAN'TS.

The Day of Tears

By Mayra B. Guillen
Age 14
Arizona, USA

People scream
Shocked
In sorrow,
Together we died
In a state of sacredness
Blessed
Victims
"Mother," we called,
"Come save us from violence."
We died working
In the tears of the towers.
Remember this day
When your eyes feel watery and afraid
Pray and be powerful for us.
This is the symbol of our tears.
The tears you won't see
"Mother," we called again
"Come save us from this terrible dream.
We waited for your response.
Don't let us die
Let our life continue
And our hearts grow
As big as America.

America Stands

By Cinthya Vazquez
Age 15
Arizona, USA

Yes,
America still stands.
The enemy left
Blood, rubble, and tears
But he didn't destroy
Our union..
He made us
Stronger
United.
He could run
Hide
But from God he couldn't
Hide or run
God will give justice.
In justice
America Stands.

The World Was Not Made for a Tragic Morning Like This

By Jorge Santizo
Age 16
Arizona, USA

The world was helpless,
Shocked,
Bathed in hatred and disbelief.
In the rubble this morning
Many lost their lives.
After the shock blew away
There came
Sadness,
Emotion,
and
Sacrifice.
The sadness of lost lives—
The emotions of revenge and loss—
And the sacrifice to seek life under the rubble.

Tuesday, September 11, 2001

By Juana Hernández
Age 18
Arizona, USA

My heart is bleeding
Because of the
Disaster in New York.
My heart is breaking
Because of people
Suffering.
My heart is like a
Red rose dying
Because people are
Killing each other.
My heart is crying
Because of hungry children.
My heart is yelling
"Help me!
Help me to stop
The war,
The racism,
The hatred,
The killing,
The injustice,
The oppression, and
The revenge."
Will my heart

Ever heal?
Will it ever be
The same again?

7

American Quotes:
Let Freedom Ring

"Let every nation know, whether it wishes us well or ill, that we shall pay any price, bear any burden, meet any hardship, support any friend, oppose any foe to assure the survival and the success of liberty."

— John Fitzgerald Kennedy

"Great tragedy has come to us, and we are meeting it with the best that is in our country, with courage and concern for others. Because this is America. This is who we are."

— President George W. Bush
September 15, 2001

"The resolve of our great nation is being tested. But make no mistake, we will show the world that we will pass the test."

— President George W. Bush
September 11, 2001

"Tonight, we are a country awakened to danger and called to defend freedom. Our grief has turned to anger and anger to resolution. Whether we bring our enemies to justice or bring justice to our enemies, justice will be done."

— President George W. Bush
September 20, 2001

"Today, our nation saw evil, the very worst of human nature. And we responded with the best of America—with the daring of our rescue workers, with the caring for strangers and neighbors who came to give blood and help in any way they could."

— President George W. Bush
September 11, 2001

"Freedom is never more than one generation away from extinction. We didn't pass it to our children in the bloodstream. It must be fought for, protected, and handed on for them to do the same, or one day we will spend our sunset years telling our children and our children's children what it was once like in the United States where men were free."

— Ronald Reagan

"Some may try and tell us that this is the end of an era. But what they overlook is that in America, every day is a new beginning. For this is the land that has never become, but is always in the act of becoming."

— Ronald Reagan
Presidential Medal of Freedom Ceremony
The White House,
January 13, 1993

"I say to you today, my friends, that in spite of the difficulties and frustrations of the moment I still have a dream. It is a dream deeply rooted in the American dream."

— Martin Luther King, Jr.

"My blood runs red, white, and blue."

Carma Haley Shoemaker

"We the People of the United States, in Order to form a more perfect Union, establish Justice, insure domestic Tranquility, provide for the common defense, promote the general Welfare, and secure the Blessings of Liberty to ourselves and our Posterity, do ordain and establish this Constitution for the United States of America."

— The US Constitution

"I've heard it asked over and over this past week, 'Where's God in all this tragedy?' I don't know about anyone else, but I've seen God's merciful hand in several places this past week. I've seen His hand at work in the fact that the World Trade Center towers stood long enough after impact for so very many of those inside to escape down the stairs and out of the buildings, instead of falling down upon impact. I've heard civil engineers wondering a couple times how those towers stood after impact since they're not built to sustain an impact of that magnitude. But yet, they did, meaning the toll of dead and missing is estimated to be 5,000 instead of 20,000 to 50,000 as are sometimes in the towers."

— Rev. Bob Rindfuss

"We will always remember. We will always be proud. We will always be prepared, so we may always be free."

— *Ronald Reagan*

"I have a dream that one day this nation will rise up and live out the true meaning of its creed - we hold these truths to be self-evident that all men are created equal.

This will be the day, this will be the day when all of God's children will be able to sing with new meaning "My country 'tis of thee, sweet land of liberty, of thee I sing. Land where my fathers died, land of the Pilgrim's pride, from every mountainside, let freedom ring!"

"And when this happens, when we allow freedom to ring, when we let it ring from every tenement and every hamlet, from every state and every city, we will be able to speed up that day when all of God's children, black men and white men, Jews and Gentiles, Protestants and Catholics, will be able to join hands and sing in the words of the old Negro spiritual, "Free at last, free at last. Thank God Almighty, we are free at last!"

— *Martin Luther King, Jr.*

"I only regret that I have but one life to lose for my country."

— *Nathan Hale, last words*
September 22, 1776

"Like an unchecked cancer, hate corrodes the personality and eats away its vital unity. Hate destroys a man's sense of values and his objectivity. It causes him to describe the beautiful as ugly and the ugly as beautiful, and to confuse the true with the false and the false with the true."

— Martin Luther King, Jr.

"The strength of the Constitution lies entirely in the determination of each citizen to defend it. Only if every single citizen feels duty bound to do his share in this defense are the constitutional rights secure."

— Albert Einstein

"You can't separate peace from freedom because no one can be at peace unless he has his freedom."

— Malcolm X

"You must not lose faith in humanity. Humanity is an ocean; if a few drops of the ocean are dirty, the ocean does not become dirty."

— Mahatma Gandhi

"One man with courage is a majority."

— *Thomas Jefferson*

"America did not invent human rights. In a very real sense, human rights invented America."

— *Jimmy Carter*

"A man who thinks of himself as belonging to a particular national group in America has not yet become an American."

— *Woodrow Wilson*

"What counts is not necessarily the size of the dog in the fight – it's the size of the fight in the dog."

— *Dwight D. Eisenhower*

"Some are born great, some achieve greatness, and some have greatness thrust upon them."

— *William Shakespeare*

"There is nothing wrong with America that the faith, love of freedom, intelligence, and energy of her citizens cannot cure."

— Dwight D. Eisenhower

"And so, my fellow Americans: Ask not what your country can do for you—ask what you can do for your country. My fellow citizens of the world: Ask not what America will do for you, but what together we can do for the freedom of man. "

— John F. Kennedy

"This is America...a brilliant diversity spread like stars, like a thousand points of light in a broad and peaceful sky. "

— George Bush

"Now, I say to you today my friends, even though we face the difficulties of today and tomorrow, I still have a dream. It is a dream deeply rooted in the American dream. I have a dream that one day this nation will rise up and live out the true meaning of its creed: 'We hold these truths to be self-evident, that all men are created equal.'"

— Martin Luther King, Jr.
August 28, 1963

"America is too great for small dreams."

— Ronald Reagan

"There is no room in this country for hyphenated Americans...The one absolutely certain way of bringing this nation to ruin, of preventing all possibility of continuing to be a nation at all would be to permit it to become a tangle of squabbling nationalities."

— Theodore Roosevelt

"Recognition of the Supreme Being is the first, the most basic, expression of Americanism. Without God, there could be no American form of government, nor American way of life."

— Dwight D. Eisenhower

"America is a tune. It must be sung together."

— Gerald Stanley Lee

"That's America for you. They won't let kids pray in school, but they put Bibles in prisons."

— Author Unknown

"There can be no fifty-fifty Americanism in this country. There is room here for only hundred-percent Americanism."

— Theodore Roosevelt

"Patriotism is easy to understand in America; it means looking out for yourself by looking out for your country."

— Calvin Coolidge

"Peace and justice are two sides of the same coin."

— Dwight D. Eisenhower

"Freedom is not free."

— Martin Luther King, Jr.

"From 40 to 60 percent of the presidential office is not in administration but in morals, politicis, and spiritual leadership...As President of the United States and servant of God, he has much more to do than to run a desk at the head of the greatest corporation in the world. He has to guide a people in the greatest adventure ever undertaken on the planet."

— *William Allen White*

"I have been driven many times to my knees by the overwhelming conviction that I had nowhere else to go. My own wisdom, and that of all about me seemed insufficient for the day."

— *Abraham Lincoln*

Be still, sad heart, and cease repining,
Behind the clouds the sun is shining;
Thy fate is the common fate of all;
Into each life some rain must fall,
Some days must be dark and dreary.

— *Henry Wadsworth Longfellow*

"Rejoice with them that do rejoice, and weep with them that weep."

— *The Bible*

"We have to condemn publicly the very idea that some people have the right to repress others. In keeping silent about evil, in burying it so deep within us that no sign of it appears on the surface, we are implanting it, and it will rise up a thousandfold in the future. When we neither punish nor reproach evildoers...we are ripping the foundations of justice from beneath new generations."

— Alexander I. Solzhenitsyn

"Never yield your courage—your courage to live, your courage to fight, to resist, to develop your own lives, to be free. I'm talking about resistance to wrong and fighting oppression."

— Roger Baldwin

"I've never been one who thought the Lord should make life easy; I've just asked Him to make me strong."

— Eva Bowring

"Out of suffering have emerged the strongest souls; the most massive characters are sheared with scars."

— E. H. Chapin

"Although the world is full of suffering, it is full also of the overcoming of it."

— Helen Keller

"No one can terrorize a whole nation unless we are all his accomplices."

— Edward R. Murrow

"Alone we can do so little; together we can do so much."

— Helen Keller

"Tragedy warms the soul, elevates the heart, can and ought to create heroes."

— Napoleon Bonaparte

"The cost of freedom is always high, but Americans have always paid it. And one path we shall never choose, and that is the path of surrender, or submission."

— John F. Kennedy

"We hold these truths to be self-evident, that all men are created equal, that they are endowed by their Creator with certain unalienable rights, that among these are life, liberty and the pursuit of happiness."

— Declaration of Independence

"America! America! God shed his grace on thee. And crown thy good with brotherhood, From sea to shining sea!"

— America the Beautiful
By Katharine Lee Bates, 1893

"I'm proud to be an American
where at least I know I'm free,
And I won't forget the men who died
who gave that right to me,
And I gladly stand up next to you
and defend her still today,
'Cause there ain't no doubt I love this land
God Bless the USA"

— God Bless the USA
By Lee Greenwood

"I pledge allegiance to the flag
of the United States of America
and to the Republic for which it stands,
one nation under God,
indivisible,
with liberty
and justice for all."

— The Pledge of Allegiance

"Oh, say can you see, by the dawn's early light,
What so proudly we hailed at the twilight's last gleaming?
Whose broad stripes and bright stars, through the perilous
fight,
O'er the ramparts we watched, were so gallantly streaming?
And the rockets' red glare, the bombs bursting in air,
Gave proof through the night that our flag was still there.
Oh, say, does that star-spangled banner yet wave
O'er the land of the free and the home of the brave?

— The Star Spangled Banner
By Francis Scott Key
September 20, 1814

"God Bless America
Land that I love
Stand beside her, and guide her
Through the night with a light from above
From the mountains, to the prairies
To the oceans, white with foam
God bless America
My home, sweet home
God bless America
My home, sweet home."

— God Bless America
By Irving Berlin, 1938

God Bless the USA

And all Freedom Loving

People of the World!

Contributor's Bios

Kari Abate is a wife, mother, poet, and photographer. She and her family live in Springfield, Illinois. Her poem is dedicated to every parent who lost a son or daughter in the terrorist attacks. She can be reached at kja@rightbrainvisions.com

Mary M. Alward lives in southern Ontario, Canada. Her work has appeared in *Chocolate for a Woman's Blessings, Chocolate for a Woman's Dreams,* and the *Sharing the Earth* series that was published by Guideposts. Mary also writes for online venues and is the Travel Center Manager at Suite101.com. E-mail: dalward@sprint.ca

Nancy Baker retired from Texas A&M University in College Station, Texas, in 1999, where she was a program coordinator in leadership training. Since retirement she has pursued her life-long love of writing and has published stories in the *Cup of Comfort* series and national magazines. She is currently working on a biography of her grandmother, entitled *Laura.*

Stefani Barbero, writer and multimedia producer, specializes in historical and documentary projects. Email: Stefani.Barbero@verizon.net

Alaine Benard writes inspirational and AD/HD-related columns. She and her twin sister also pen a humorous advice series. She has co-authored two anthologies, with three more in the works. Her AD/HD book is scheduled for publication by the end of 2002. Benard's award-winning *StormWatch* newsletter and contact information is located at: www.dixiesky.com/ADHD_Soaring

Kymberli W. Brady, is an author, artist, and photographer who has received numerous television credits and awards. She has written two books. *Give Them Wings and Let Them Fly* deals with surviving the loss of a child. *The Sleepy Little Star* celebrates the light and love of children everywhere. For more information, visit: www.givethemwings.com and www.kymzinn.com or email her at: gtgrphc@aol.com.

Julie Weed Brendel was born in Los Angeles, California, and currently resides in Indiana. She has been married for 23 years and has two teenage children. Julie owns a day spa and travels all over the world doing hair and makeup for prestigious award shows. She is currently working on her first novel.

Flor Cardona is 20 years old. She's a member of the Hopi Foundation's CPRV Owl and Panther program. She is currently writing a picture book about a refugee from Guatemala, her homeland. Flor recently attended the June 2002 "Abolish Torture" Conference in Washington, D.C.

Shelle Castles is a freelance writer and a former reporter for her hometown weekly newspaper. She strives for the title of "novelist" and hopes to make that title become a reality one day. She wishes for God's blessings on our hero's and victims of 9/11. Email: swriter@netdoor.com Website: www.writecastles.8k.com

Garry Chartier is a columnist with *Sunday Magazine*, a non-denominational Christian publication based in Victoria, British Columbia, Canada. His poems, columns, and other articles have been published in various magazines and newspapers. Garry and his wife live in Nanaimo on Vancouver Island in Canada.

Jolene Coiner is the 27 year old mother of three children ages 11, 8, and newborn. She writes articles on subjects such as teen pregnancy and single parenting from her own life experiences. In her spare time she likes making crafts, spending time with family, and writing poetry.

Mary Lane Cryns ("Melody") is a writer and single mom with four kids who lives in Porterville, California with her two younger children. She is a member of Momwriters and the International Women Writing Guild and writes fiction, folksy essays, and stories about family life adventures. Email: melodywrites@sosinet.net

Kathleen Cyr is a freelance writer, wife, and mother of two. Her personal essays have appeared in several online publications. She is the Editor of www.thewritersgallery.com and the Emotional Abuse Coordinator and Teen Editor/Advisor for www.apeaceoflife.com. In her spare time, she loves to read and spend time with her family.

Jim Donovan is an author, coach, and inspirational speaker. His books, including his latest, *Reclaim Your Life,* have been read throughout the world and he has become a major force in the field of personal growth. Jim's articles and a free subscription to his newsletter are available from www.jimdonovan.com

Traci Amor Draper lives in Springtown, California, with her husband, Marty, and her children, Jared,—whose story is also included in this book—Erika, and Starr. Traci has been writing since the third grade when she won her first writing contest. She is currently working on three novels. Email: tamor@attbi.com Website: www.inkthoughts.com

Raynette Eitel grew up in the Southwest, a poet even in childhood. Her poetry has been published in newspapers, literary publications, and professional journals. She is now retired in Las Vegas and continues to write. Her poems, "The Day the Planes Quit Flying" and "Grieve, America" were read in many benefit shows for 9/11 victims. She is a graduate of Colorado College and the University of Colorado.

Teraisa Goldman has written hundreds of articles for publications such as *Woman's Day, Baby Years,* and *Highlights For Children,* and is now completing *The U-Haul Murders: True Crime and Capital Punishment* and has a screenplay in circulation. When not writing, she home schools her three girls. Website: www.GetItInWriting.org

Catherine C. Harris makes her home in North Carolina where she enjoys slow country living with her husband and three children. Catherine enjoys writing about life experiences, self-esteem issues, and various other topics related to diversity. Catherine manages a website devoted to the acceptance of diversity at www.positiveperfectyou.com

Karen Hawkins is a freelance writer and craft designer. She lives on a 6 1/2-acre farm in Southwestern Maine that is home to a variety of critters and children. For more information, visit her online at www.offthewallemporium.com

Margaret Helmstetter is a freelance writer who lives in Arizona surrounded by her family and assorted pets. She is the assistant editor at http://www.childcare-sentinal.com, published by Provider Press. She writes about the things she loves—children, family, and pets.

Mae Hochstetler lives in Youngstown, Ohio, with her husband, Marcus, and their four children—all under five years old. A graduate of Ashland University, Mae is the At-Large Board member for the Synodical Women's Organization (ELCA) of Northeast Ohio and the Computers for Shelters Coordinator for www.apeaceoflife.com

Joyce Jace is a full-time freelance writer, syndicated columnist, and up-and-coming author. Her autobiography, *I Don't Care, I'm Finally an Author* was released in 2002. Visit her on the Web at www.jmjace.com

Shirley Kawa-Jump is the author of several books, including *The Virgin's Proposal* (Silhouette Romance, January 2003) and *How to Publish Your Articles* (Square One Publishers, September 2001). A mother of two and caretaker of too many pets to count, she divides her time between writing and carpooling. More information can be found on www.writingcorner.com

David Koy has written more than 180 stories and articles that have been published in the *Milwaukee Journal, Wausau Daily Herald, Wisconsin Christian News, Spotlight Magazine*, and other periodicals. He also received a $1000 cash award from the Amy Foundation in 2000 for his *Wausau Daily Herald* article entitled, "To stop killings, make God priority."

Trina Lambert is a Colorado-based writer, volunteer, wife, and mother. She honed her earliest writing skills in letters sent to pen pals and other friends. Her essays and commentaries have appeared in *TWINS Magazine*, Moms Online, and the *Denver Post*. Learn more about her at: www.trinalambert.com

Cathy Laska is a writer from Wausau, Wisconsin, who aspires to become a full-time freelancer. She enjoys writing poetry and essays about her missionary trip to Africa and would like to compile them in a book one day.

Dari Lavender is a former news reporter and columnist for the *Calhoun News/Dispatch* and former features writer for the *Dalton Advertiser*. She is now a freelance writer and a member of *The Sowers Syndicate*, whose mission matches her own: to provide well written, upbeat, and energizing writing from a Christian perspective. www.SowerS.com

Kathryn Lay lives in Texas with her husband and daughter. Her work has appeared in *Woman's Day, Guideposts, Home Life, Chicken Soup For The Mother's Soul, God Allows U-Turns Vol. 1, Highlights for Children, Healthy Child Care, Woman's World,* and hundreds more. She can be reached at rlay15@aol.com.

Mary Dixon Lebeau is a freelance writer and employment counselor who lives with her husband and her children (Courtney, Steven, Sean, and Max) in West Deptford, New Jersey. Her weekly column appears in The Gloucester County (NJ) Times. Mary may be reached at mweidler@snip.net

Shannon Leigh is a promising new contemporary country/pop singer/songwriter. Her voice carries a unique blend of power, passion, and soul. She is currently recording her first CD, to include Destination: Heaven. You can learn more about Shannon at her website, www.shannon-leigh.com

Angie Ledbetter is the mother of three, step-mom of two, and grandmother ("Nana") to two. She stays busy with ministry work, scouts, and writing. Angie writes inspirational and humor/advice columns, is co-authoring an inspirational book series, and writes for ezines and print publications. Her writing site is at: www.dixiesky.com/writersgumbo

Jennifer LB Leese is a mom from Maryland. In 2001, her children's book *Sounds I Hear* was nominated for the EPIC EPPIE Award; that same book hit #3 on the children's ebook bestseller list. Mrs. Leese makes up one-half of the fantasy, horror author JV Harlee. Email: AStoryWeaver@aol.com Website: www.geocities.com/ladyjiraff/writers.html

Kyle Looby studied writing and the teaching of writing at Southern Illinois University and the University of Illinois where she received her M.A. Looby has written for *Writer Online, Writer's Block, The Electronic Writer, Writers-Exchange, The Writing Parent, Absolute Write, Inscriptions*, and *Freelance Success*, as well as many non-writing publications.

Sharon M. Thompson Loomis is a single mom of three: Michael, 9; William, 6; and Mackenzie, 5. In 1987, she graduated from Cypress Lake High School in Ft. Myers, FL and joined the US Navy where she served 4 years at NAS Barbers Point, Hawaii. She currently resides in La Crosse, Wisconsin.

Gwen Morrison is a freelance writer and mom of four children ages 5 through 17. She has definitely "been there, done that." Gwen claims that her family life alone could keep her in material for decades. Her work can be seen online and in print in various publications.

V.K. Mullins lives in Michigan with her husband and three children. She has written for her local newspaper, been published on several websites, and written two books. She is a founding member of the Southeastern Michigan Writers Association. Contact her at vkm49@aol.com

April O'Herron is an Ohio writer who now realizes that there isn't enough time left to write all the things she wants to write. She'll be spending the rest of her life trying to catch up. You can contact her at aprilsphere@yahoo.com

Heather O'Neil is a freelance writer and artist in Ontario, Canada. Previously a newspaper columnist for a local paper, Heather is presently putting together a series of cookbooks with her own brand of down home cooking. When time permits, she relaxes with her bead box and constructs beautiful, one-of-a-kind rosaries, chaplets, and prayer beads.

Michelle Pearson is a freelance writer and home-based business owner who lives with her husband and son on a fifth-generation family farm in northwestern Illinois. Her work has appeared in *God Allows U-Turns* and *Chocolate for a Woman's Soul* as well as regional and national publications. Website: www.countrymeadowsoapworks.com

Crystel Riggs is a wife, mother, small business owner, and writer. Her husband and children are her life. Business is her entertainment. Writing is her therapy. It is her dream to someday write something that will make a difference in the life of at least one person.

Barbara Jane Russell Robinson teaches sixth, seventh, and eighth graders at Denn John Middle school in Kissimmee, Florida. She's a member of the Florida Writer's Association, author of *Magnolia: A Wilting Flower* soon to make its debut at www.publishamerica.com and author of "My Special Mother" in *Mothers of Writers* available at Publish America. Website: www.pages.prodigy.net/bud25.

Shannon Roudebush and her husband, Brad, reside in Westfield, Indiana, where they own and operate an erosion control business. This year they are expecting two blessings from God: one adopted daughter from China and one birth child. Shannon enjoys yoga, reading, and scrapbooking.

M. J. Rose is the author of the novels, *Lip Service* (PocketBooks1999), and *In Fidelity* (PocketBooks 2000). Her third novel, *Letting Go* (Ballantine 2002) will be released in July 2002. Rose is also the co-author of *How to Publish and Promote Online* (St. Martin's Press 2000. Email: mjroseauthor@aol.com Website: www.mjrose.com

April Lee Schmidt is a freelance writer originally from Michigan's upper peninsula. She currently resides with her husband, an E.M.T./L.P.N., and their three youngest children in west central Alabama.

Sue Shackles is a freelance writer living in Washington state with her husband, two children, and a zoo. Her articles have appeared in local publications and on the Internet. She is presently working on a book dealing with Internet safety for teens. You can reach Sue at: SueShackles@centurytel.net Website: www.womenonwriting/sueshackles

Bea Sheftel is published in several anthologies including *Guideposts, Listening to the Animals; Chicken Soup for the Nurses Soul, I Bring You Glad Tidings, The Recovering Catholic,* and *God Allows U Turns.* Her ebooks are *The Writing Plan* and *Preserving Your Memories in a Scrapbook.* Her memoir is *From Brooklyn with Love.* Email: bts1ct@aol.com Website: www.memoirwritersonline.com

Carma Haley Shoemaker, whose true passion is poetry, hopes to one day have her name on the cover of numerous children's books, song lyric sheets, and CD covers. Her writing can be seen in *Baby Years Magazine; Pregnancy Magazine*; or at iParenting.com. Visit her website at www.CarmasWords.com

Margaret Byers Smith received her bachelors magna cum laude at San Diego State in psychology and did advanced work at USIU, San Diego, California. She taught at Imperial Valley College, California; Missouri Southern State; High Point College, North Carolina; and Northwest Arkansas Community College. She's been published in academia, women's magazines, and online.

Rebecca Spence is a published researcher, author, and mother of two young daughters. Making her debut as a children's book author last spring with the publication of *Little Mouse*, (©2001, from Little Iris Press), Rebecca also holds an M.B.A. from Harvard Business School and works as a marketing consultant.

Paul Spreadbury lives in Maine with his wife and daughter. Two Thousand One, Nine Eleven was written so that children, especially those directly affected by the attack, could understand that the sacrifice made by those who died in the attack helped to create the re-United States of America. Paul enjoys golf—*a lot.* Email: bbeesboy@earthlink.net

Mary E. Tyler lives in Newport News, Virginia, with her husband and three daughters. She is the owner of The Write Element, a copywriting service and Private Ice Publications, a niche publisher of sports fiction. Romantic Times called her book, *On the Edge,* "An excellent story with marvelous characters."

Shannon Walker lives in Fort Myers, Florida, with her 8-year-old daughter, Jade—whose story also appears in this book. Shannon is an avid photographer who also enjoys writing poetry and short stories.

Victoria Walker is a freelance writer living in Fort Myers, Florida. Her work has appeared in numerous books, magazines, and websites including *Chicken Soup for the Soul of America, Wonder Years, and EcoFlorida Magazine.* Email: victoria@victoriawalker.com   Website: www.VictoriaWalker.com

Lori Williams is a poet and born and bred New Yorker. She was in Florida on September 11th, contemplating a move there. The events of that day made her realize that New York was more than just a place to live—it was home. Her tribute website can be found at www.loriwilliams.homestead.com/mybeautifulnewyork.html.

Shirley Ann Walker Young lives in Valdosta, Georgia. She was born in Lake City, Florida, and grew up in a little town in Georgia called Echols County. Shirley is thankful for many things in life, most importantly her husband, Rickey, and their three beautiful children, Brittany, Rickey, Jr., and Bridget.

CHILDREN

Miguel Agosto is an eighth grader at Denn John Middle School in Kissimmee, Florida, and a member of the creative writing club, Denn John Writing Dragons. Miguel had his first poem about his mother published as a seventh grader. Miguel's writings appear in *Denn John Writing Dragons on the Roller Coaster of Life.*

Jared Amor is 10 years old and in the fourth grade. He lives in Springtown, California, with his mother, Traci; father, Marty; sisters, Erika, 5, and Starr, 2. He is very active in school and loves to write.

Giovanni Aponte is a sixth grader at Denn John Middle School in Kissimmee, Florida. He has two older brothers and a sister and is proud of the fact that he is writing a lot this year. He was recently interviewed by a reporter from the *Osceola News Gazette* at a creative writing club meeting.

Turner Benard is a 10-year-old honor roll student at St. Gerard Majella Catholic Elementary in Baton Rouge, Louisiana. He plays football and basketball and loves creative writing, drawing, and his rat terrier, Jinx.

Jennifer Cruz is a 12-year-old Guatemalan who likes school very much. She would like to be a doctor in the future so she can help people to get well. She is in the Hopi Foundation's CPRV Owl and Panther writing program.

Moslin Cruz is 10-year-old Guatemalan who has one sister. His goal is to go the university and become an engineer. His favorite thing to do at home is creating experiments in science. He is a member of the Hopi Foundation's CPRV Owl and Panther writing program.

MyKaela Korryn Edrich is a very impressionable seven-year-old who loves life, dressing in her brother's clothes, calling her Nana, and writing.

Maureen Gard is an eighth grader at Lundahl Middle School in Crystal Lake, Illinois. She plays trumpet and is involved in school plays, chorus, jazz band, and basketball. Maureen has a passion for animals and wants to have a career as a veterinarian. Writing poems about animals is her first love.

Mayra Guillen is a Sophomore at Tucson High School, Arizona. Her dream is to learn sign language and work with the deaf. She was born in Veracruz, Mexico. She loves poetry and playing with creative words. She is a member of the Hopi Foundation's CPRV Owl and Panther program.

Brianna Hardy is 11 years old. At the time of the terrorist attack on the U.S., she was a fifth grader attending Kate Goodrich Elementary School. She will be a sixth grader at Prairie River Middle School in Merrill, Wisconsin, in September 2002.

Juana Hernandez is from Guatemala. Her native indigenous language is Quiche. She is also fluent in Spanish and English. Juana is a graduating senior from Tucson High School in Arizona and hopes to begin college and study to become a nurse. Her favorite pastime is listening to music. She is a member of the Hopi Foundation's CPRV Owl and Panther program.

Katarina Beth Miller is nine years old and lives in Merrill, Wisconsin. She likes to write and read and go to camp. She attends Trinity Lutheran School in Merrill and is going into the fifth grade.

Stephanie Ortiz is an eighth grader at Denn John Middle School in Kissimmee, Florida. Stephanie has strong feelings related to September 11 since it took place on her birthday. Some of her writings will be published in *Denn John Writing Dragons on the Roller Coaster of Life*, a student-produced paperback.

Jeremy Pedelose attends Denn John Middle School in Kissimmee   where he likes to socialize with his peers and write. He was interviewed by a reporter earlier this year when the reporter covered a creative-writing club meeting, and the first lines of Jeremy's poem were in the *Osceola Sentinel.*

Jolene Plummer is seven years old. She lives in Merrill, Wisconsin, and likes to play soccer. She will be in the second grade at Kate Goodrich Elementary School in the fall of 2002.

Alfonso Reyes is nine years old and is in third grade. Alfonso's parents are from El Salvador and Mexico. He was part of the Hopi Foundation CPRV's Owl and Panther writing program before he could read. Alfonso is an exceptional artist. He would like to go to outer space.

Jorge Santizo will be a Senior this fall at Palo Verde High School. He hopes to get a scholarship to attend the University of Arizona and get a degree in engineering. He came with his parents and sister at age four to escape from death and war in Guatemala. He is a member of the Hopi Foundation's CPRV Owl and Panther program.

Amy Shackles is a seventh grader from Washington State. She is a fledgling science fiction writer and avid reader. An honor student, she also plays basketball and competes in the school Knowledge Bowl. She is presently working on her first full-length sci-fi novel. Email Amy at: Britqueeni@aol.com

Cody Shoemaker is a sixth grader who is very active in soccer, baseball, and band at his middle school. Cody is also involved in several organizations and has been making and giving away ribbons, paper flags, and handmade red, white, and blue bookmarks to help show his support of America following the 9-11 tragedy.

Rob Shoemaker is a first grade student in North Carolina where he also plays soccer and baseball. Rob has been helping his older brother hand out paper flags in his neighborhood for people to hang in the windows of their homes and cars.

Cinthya Vasquez is 16 years old and from Mexico. She hopes to be a police officer. She will be a Junior at Pueblo High School this fall. She loves to write cute poems about her life. She is a member of the Hopi Foundation's CPRV Owl and Panther program.

Jade Alana Walker is eight years old and a member of Major Work Area, a program for gifted students, at Three Oaks Elementary School. She lives in Fort Myers, Florida, with her mom, Shannon. Jade enjoys all kinds of crafts—drawing, making projects, and writing stories.

Permissions:

About the Author
who compiled this book

Photo Provided

Victoria Walker was born in Valdosta, Georgia, and relocated to Fort Myers, Florida, at the age of eight. After seeking exciting adventures living in Charleston, South Carolina; Orlando, Florida; and Denver, Colorado—she returned home to Fort Myers, Florida, where she resides with her teenage son, Jeremy.

Her dream is to write best sellers from a mountainside chalet—somewhere in the beautiful state of Tennessee.

Her writing has been published in numerous books, magazines, and websites.

Visit Victoria online at www.victoriawalker.com.

Order Other Books Published by:

OBADIAH PRESS

Qty. Ordered

___**Running As Fast As I Can@** $16.95
by Lois Hilton Spoon

Exactly one year from the day she was told she would die from terminal cancer, Lois ran a ten mile race, and she hasn't slowed down since. A story of hope, God's miraculous intervention, and life, the stories from this book will fly from the pages into your heart.

___**Good Mourning, Lord@** $15.95
by Alyice Edrich

When her child died, a part of Alyice did, too. Raw and emotionally poignant, she shares her feelings and provides room for you to journal your own feelings as you work through *your* grief, knowing there is no "right way" to grieve.

___**When A Woman Prays@** $15.95
by Tina L. Miller

Miracles can happen when a woman prays...Tap into the power of prayer and change your life. Develop your own very personal, intimate relationship with God and fill your soul with His peace...Discover the power of prayer in your life and be blessed!

Total for books ordered above = $_____
___# of books ordered x $2 S/H per book = $_____
TOTAL = $_____

VISA
MasterCard

☐ My check or money order is enclosed. **OR**
☐ Please charge my Mastercard or VISA
My credit card number is: ——————————
It expires on: _____ My name exactly as shown on my credit card is: _____

_____   _____
Signature   Date

Mail your order to:

Obadiah Press
607 N. Cleveland St.
Merrill, WI 54452

Fax: 715-536-3167

Or Call
Toll Free:
1-866-536-3167

Ship Books to:
Name_____
Address_____
_____

Prices shown are US funds. Include $2 additional for Canadian orders and $4 additional for other international orders. Quantity discounts available. Write for information. This form may be freely reproduced.

OBADIAH PRESS
A Christian Publishing House

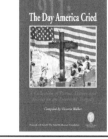

Order Form

Please send ____ copies of *911: The Day America Cried* to:

911: The Day America Cried
compiled by Victoria Walker
ISBN 0-9713266-5-7

Name: _____

Address: _____

City: _____ State: _____

Zip: _____

Country: _____

Telephone: _____

Book Price: $15.95 in U.S. dollars

Shipping & Handling: $2.00 in U.S. dollars per book
(Include $2 additional for Canadian orders and $4 additional
for other international orders.)

☐ My check or money order is enclosed. **OR**
☐ Please charge my Mastercard or VISA
    My credit card number is: _____
    It expires on: _____ My name exactly as shown on
    my credit card is:_____

VISA

MasterCard

_____   _____
Signature   Date

Mail your order to:
    Obadiah Press
    607 N. Cleveland Street
    Merrill, WI 54452

Or Fax to: 715-536-3167

**Or Call
Toll Free:
1-866-536-3167**

Quantity discounts available. Write for information.
This form may be freely reproduced.

OBADIAH PRESS
A Christian Publishing House

Order Form

| Good Mourning, Lord |
| by Alyice Edrich |
| ISBN 0-9713266-4-9 |

Please send ____ copies of *Good Mourning, Lord* by Alyice Edrich to:

Name: _____

Address: _____

City: _____ State: _____

Zip: _____

Country: _____

Telephone: _____

Book Price: $15.95 in U.S. dollars

Shipping & Handling: $2.00 in U.S. dollars per book
(Include $2 additional for Canadian orders and $4 additional for other international orders.)

☐ My check or money order is enclosed. **OR**
☐ Please charge my Mastercard or VISA
  My credit card number is: _____
  It expires on: _____ My name exactly as shown on
  my credit card is:_____

VISA

MasterCard

_____   _____
Signature   Date

Mail your order to:
  Obadiah Press
  607 N. Cleveland Street
  Merrill, WI 54452

Or Fax to: 715-536-3167

**Or Call
Toll Free:
1-866-536-3167**

Quantity discounts available. Write for information.
This form may be freely reproduced.

OBADIAH PRESS
A Christian Publishing House

Order Form

Please send ___ **copies of** *Running As Fast As I Can* **by Lois Hilton Spoon to:**

> *Running As Fast As I Can*
> by Lois Hilton Spoon
> ISBN 0-9713266-0-6

Name: _____

Address: _____

City: _____ State: _____

Zip: _____

Country: _____

Telephone: _____

Book Price: $16.95 in U.S. dollars

Shipping & Handling: $2.00 in U.S. dollars per book
(Include $2 additional for Canadian orders and $4 additional for other international orders.)

☐ My check or money order is enclosed. **OR**
☐ Please charge my Mastercard or VISA
  My credit card number is: _____
  It expires on: _____ My name exactly as shown on
  my credit card is:_____

VISA

MasterCard

_____   _____
Signature   Date

Mail your order to:
    Obadiah Press
    607 N. Cleveland Street
    Merrill, WI 54452

Or Fax to: 715-536-3167

**Or Call
Toll Free:
1-866-536-3167**

Quantity discounts available. Write for information.
This form may be freely reproduced.

OBADIAH PRESS
A Christian Publishing House

Order Form

Please send ____ copies of *When A Woman Prays* by Tina L. Miller to:

When A Woman Prays
by Tina L. Miller
ISBN 0-9713266-1-4

Name: _____

Address: _____

City: _____State: _____

Zip: _____

Country: _____

Telephone: _____

Book Price: $15.95 in U.S. dollars

Shipping & Handling: $2.00 in U.S. dollars per book
(Include $2 additional for Canadian orders and $4 additional for other international orders.)

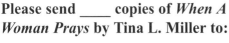

☐ My check or money order is enclosed. **OR**
☐ Please charge my Mastercard or VISA
  My credit card number is: _____
  It expires on: _____ My name exactly as shown on
  my credit card is:_____

_____   _____
Signature   Date

Mail your order to:
  Obadiah Press
  607 N. Cleveland Street
  Merrill, WI 54452

Or Fax to: 715-536-3167

**Or Call
Toll Free:
1-866-536-3167**

Quantity discounts available. Write for information.

OBADIAH MAGAZINE

For People Who Live Their Lives to Love and Serve the Lord

Just $15 for 4 quarterly issues!

Canadian subscriptions: $18
Other International subscriptions: $20

Subscribe Me!

Mail To: Obadiah Magazine
c/o Obadiah Press
1826 Crossover Road, PMB 108
Fayetteville, AR 72703

Name: _____

Address: _____

_____

City, State, Zip: _____

Country: _____ Phone: _____

Include check or money order (US funds) for each subscription ordered.

Initial Subscription: _____ Renewal: _____ (check one)

Did anyone refer you to Obadiah Magazine? If so, please include their name here. They may be eligible to win a $100 prize in our "Most Subscription Referrals Contest."

_____

Send a Gift Subscriptio

Mail To: Obadiah Magazine
c/o Obadiah Press
1826 Crossover Road, PMB 108
Fayetteville, AR 72703

Please send a gift subscription TO:

Name: _____

Address: _____

_____

City, State, Zip: _____

Country: _____ Phone: _____

FROM: _____

NOTE TO INCLUDE WITH FIRST ISSUE: _____

_____

_____

Include check or money order (US funds) for each subscription ordered.

This form may be freely reproduced.